Still your grandfather's AA? ... Layne makes clear that alcoholism is still widely considered to be a moral failure that requires a moral solution. He then calmly suggests that the frantic seeking of solutions outside ourselves is not necessarily the answer.

— John B. Henderson NV

Removing the mysticism, Wes has written the "how's and why's of the 12-Step program" as 'a model for living,' suggested by Bill W.

— Keith T., sober member of AA for 44 years

A large number of AA members regard the Big Book as an infallible text. Wes Layne is among a large number of folks who recognize that parts of that book simply cannot be absolutely true—and here is the crucial bit, right or wrong—all of it is open to questioning. Wes's credo is to question everything, and he questions a lot in this book.

— Kurt R, Las Vegas NV

Wes Layne has no quarrel with those who find comfort in the "Big Book," often treated as word-for-word divine scripture by traditionalists; nor does he take issue with Christian theology. He merely offers a clear-eyed examination of those themes in the "Big Book" that can bring confusion to a Westerner like me who intuits a truth—a reality beyond the confines of a fundamentally biblical, religious culture.

— Matt H. Las Vegas NV

A book thoughtfully written that should be read thoughtfully.

I'm hoping that this book reaches those who are still struggling, not only with their alcoholism, but with the "solution" that would take them down the traditional avenues. Wes would be adamant about the fact that his experiences do not define "the" way, his description of them merely suggests that there is another way.

Perhaps the most important message here is that if you suspect that your solution may be "outside the box", you are not alone.

Not a "how to" book, but a "what happened" series of essays of enlightening text. Layne shows the early mechanics of getting sober, then staying sober, and the ultimate result: simply being sober. Which in its essence is, The Tao of Sobriety.

THE
TAO OF
SOBRIETY

A JOURNEY OF RECOVERY
THROUGH AND BEYOND
ALCOHOLICS ANONYMOUS

WES LAYNE

This book is intended to provide accurate information with regard to its subject matter and reflects the opinion and perspective of the author. However, in times of rapid change, ensuring all information provided is entirely accurate and up-to-date at all times is not always possible. Therefore, the author and publisher accept no responsibility for inaccuracies or omissions and specifically disclaim any liability, loss or risk, personal, professional or otherwise, which may be incurred as a consequence, directly or indirectly, of the use and/or application of any of the contents of this book.

TABLE OF CONTENTS

PREFACE

I SPENT NEARLY MY ENTIRE working life in the building trades. I sometimes jokingly point out that I had considered myself to be superintendent material from the moment I pounded that first nail; however, it wasn't until after I had gotten sober in 1990 that I began to find employers who agreed with me.

That career ended abruptly in 2009 as the world-wide financial crisis brought construction in Las Vegas to a complete standstill. At that time the only thing that was on my bucket list that I could afford to do was to get deeply involved in Alcoholics Anonymous again and that is precisely how I began to spend a lot of my new-found free time.

Superficially that would seem to be adequately described by the significant increase in my meeting attendance, as well as my working with several newer members. Outside of that physical presence, however, I found that the abundance of free time also allowed me to get involved in a much deeper investigation into my own experiences of being sober and how profoundly that had influenced my life.

I began to spend a significant amount of time in the aspects of a meditation practice that involve contemplation and inquiry. What I began to realize more than ever before was that even though my world view had been influenced significantly by my participation in AA, that world view was neither concurrent with the world view of most of the folks that I knew in AA, nor with the rigidity and the structure of traditional AA.

As I began to identify specific details of those differing perspectives, I began to write some of those details down– simply "notes to self" I suppose. Over time, and as I occasionally reviewed those notes, I began to recognize that some of those notes could be organized into themes, and that with a little effort I could actually write intelligible essays that could describe and help explain the differences as well as the commonalities of those various opinions. I began to do just that.

The Tao of Sobriety is a collection of those essays. Unlike dozens of books that offer alternative methods or paths to sobriety, these essays point out the usefulness of many of the resources that have always been fundamental to the success of AA. Unlike traditional points of view however, I point out that *being* sober is beyond the mechanics of getting sober and staying sober. It is the result of continuing the process of what Bill Wilson himself described as "getting down to causes and conditions." That is the fundamental theme of this collection of writings.

Traditional AA parallels the theology of Western culture and without a thorough examination of that relationship, it's easy to assume that the process is about self-improvement. In other words, proving yourself worthy of sobriety. However, if your investigation into "causes and conditions" continues and deepens, you begin to realize that it's much more about self-realization. There is an enormous difference.

While having a fundamental understanding of AA may be helpful as you read these essays, it is not essential. My intent here is to point out that the recovery of a fundamental sense of *be*-ing is far beyond the recovery from alcoholism.

On the surface these ramblings may appear to be about the drinking and then not drinking. However, they are all woven together with my perspective of the *human* dilemma and the resolution of that; a perspective that has been influenced by my participation in Alcoholics Anonymous as well as my own personal spiritual practice. A practice that has evolved over the past several decades and one that continues to evolve– in no small part as the result of my continuing that participation.

One final note here: I don't share my thoughts because I think it will change the minds of those that think differently.... I share my thoughts to show the people who already think like me that they are not alone.

Wes Layne
Summer 2023

THE MOST FUNDAMENTAL OF QUESTIONS: "IS THIS ALL THERE IS?"

This piece is about my perspective of the evolution of Alcoholics Anonymous as it progressed from its humble beginnings to the essence of what it Is today. I have attempted to be as factual as possible regarding the historical details. As always though, all that I present here is interspersed with my opinions.

IMAGINE A PAIR OF OUR ancient ancestors sitting on a rock one afternoon after a particularly arduous day of hunting and/or gathering, and one of them, with his head hung low, wistfully asking his companion, "Is this all there is?"

"Boy I sure hope not," is the reply.

"What do mean by *hope*?" asks the first one cocking his head sideways to look at his friend.

"Come on man use your imagination!" the other one replies as he stands up and spreads his arms wide. "This is probably _____ but if _____, then _____."

I'll let you fill in the blanks. The point is that in that instant, hope as they say, sprang eternal and began to serve as the ultimate panacea for their underlying fear.

The hope that the future will somehow be different is undoubtedly the most common way of avoiding the uncomfortable reality of the present.

One of the more interesting things about hope is that when it is fervent enough, hope eventually solidifies into belief, especially as it is shared with, and embellished by, others.

It would seem likely that early humans began to ponder deep philosophical questions as soon as their cognitive abilities evolved to the point of having the capacity to ask them. As they began to gather in groups, they would have undoubtedly begun to compare notes, and the gradual arrival at some sort of consensus would have been the foundation for each group's origin story. As time passed, these myths and their accompanying deities became an integral part of the fabric of the various cultures that were beginning to emerge.

There have been innumerable volumes written by cultural anthropologists, evolutionary theorists, and others, that speculate about every detail of the evolution of the human species as well as the evolution of our many different cultures. One of the things I find fascinating about those studies is the ways in which myths-turned-beliefs become such a vital part of not only what binds groups of people together, but also what fosters the sense of separateness between themselves and anyone outside the group. A quick side note here: the power of belief lies not in its truth, but in the universality of its acceptance.

All that brings me to the microcosm that is the culture of Alcoholics Anonymous. When viewed through the lens of cultural evolution, AA has followed an interesting pattern.

After his meeting with Ebby, Bill must have had some hope that what Ebby described as his own solution to the drink problem might work for him as well. Otherwise, he would not have bothered with the meetings at the Calvary Mission or with the Reverend Sam Shoemaker who was preaching the fundamentalist Christian doctrine of the Oxford Group there and at the nearby Calvary Church.

Since he showed up drunk, however, Bill's first experience with the folks at the mission was a disaster, and within a few days he found himself once again in Towns Hospital, exhausted, sedated, and in as bad a shape as ever. Then, seemingly out of nowhere, came the vision!

Bill described that momentous event with differing details as time went on, and I have my own opinion about the genesis of it, but the fact remains that in his words, "the result was electric." Bill seemed to have suddenly lost not only the desire to drink, but the obsession as well.

That experience became the foundation of the origin story of Alcoholics Anonymous. Since Bill had no way to adequately describe that "white light" experience, either to himself or to anyone else, he began to use the language of Christianity that he was familiar with from his childhood. It was no coincidence that the Oxford Group spoke that same language; that's where Bill initially found his community, and where he began his search for prospects. Bill's hope that he could find a way to stay sober had been transcended by the hope that he could help others get sober.

Bill's success was minimal however, until some months later when he found himself in Akron, Ohio, out of town and out of sorts. A desperate search for another drunk to talk to resulted in his making the acquaintance of Henrietta Sieberling (a stalwart Oxford Grouper), who arranged to host a meeting the following day at her home in the Sieberling gate house. That meeting, between Bill and Dr. Bob, was another significant piece of the origin story. Bob seems to have been the first to grasp the reality of Bill's message; that it *is* possible to live a fulfilling life without alcohol, but even more importantly, that that message is most effectively communicated from one drunk to another, and perhaps most importantly that the benefits of that communication are mutual.

Bob and his wife Ann had been attending meetings of the Oxford Group for some months prior to his meeting Bill, and since Bill remained in Akron for several months, it was only natural for him to join them. As is so often the case, the culture of AA began as a subculture of an existing, and much larger, culture. For more than four years, the sober drunks in Akron remained "the alcoholic squad" of the Oxford Group. In fact, the meetings in Akron were Oxford Group meetings, held in the homes of the Oxford Group members, attended by an ever-widening assortment of drunks. There could be little doubt that the "cultural bias" of the Oxford Group found its way into the subculture of early AA there.

In New York, the situation was a bit different. Bill's initial contact with many of the early New York members had come via Towns Hospital, and most of the meetings were in Bill and Lois's home in Brooklyn. A number of these fellows were more pragmatic, and a couple of them were quite defiant about their non-belief. Following the chapter-and-verse religiosity that seemed to be running smoothly in Akron wasn't playing nearly as well in New York.

There was one constant—Bill—who by his own description was at least as derelict as most of them and who had not had a drink for nearly a year! Despite the individual differences in the preferred methods and their application, the hope was rising. The individual hopes of so many of them that had never been realized, were coalescing into a group hope; a rising tide that lifts all boats.

The cultures of Akron AA and New York AA continued to evolve but in different ways. Unlike the group in Akron, Bill and the New York group abandoned their ties with the Oxford Group in 1937. Not long afterward, Bill's suggestion that they should write a book began to raise the ire of many of the folks in Akron. I'm not sure that Dr. Bob himself was completely sold on the book idea, but most accounts suggest that he seemed to be—perhaps simply to keep peace in the family.

Even though I have some fairly strong opinions about what I consider to be the negligible contribution of the Akron members in general, and Dr. Bob in particular, to the actual founding of Alcoholics Anonymous, there is no need to explore any of that here.

What *is* worthy of some careful consideration, however, is what Bill's mindset might have been. I can only speculate, but as I review his relentless efforts, I suspect that Bill somehow intuitively sensed that what seemed to be plodding along at a snail's pace could not, and would not, survive unless it was, in a manner of speaking, "taken public."

It was toward that end that Bill focused his attention. He seemingly left no stone unturned as he approached everyone he could think of, soliciting endorsements and/or donations. He got little of either.

The details of those endeavors are not particularly pertinent, other than noting how disappointed and frustrated Bill must have been with their minimal success. It is my opinion however, that those events, which at the time were most certainly seen as setbacks, were beginning to bolster and validate Bill's inclinations about writing a book.

As time went on the book idea became his primary focus and raising support and financing for that project took center stage. The publication of the book

Alcoholics Anonymous was the final chapter in the origin story of AA.

The spectrum of opinions about the book itself is vast, ranging from the belief that Bill was just a conduit, and that the book was actually written by the hand of God his own damned self, to its dismissal as being nothing more than the outdated ramblings of a religious cultist.

It is my opinion that the book is extremely valuable, not only as a historical document, but also because it continues to define quite literally the culture of Alcoholics Anonymous as it has evolved from the date of its publication in 1939 until today. In short, AA would not exist without it.

It is also my opinion that though raising some much-needed capital to support the ongoing efforts of the organization was a motivating factor, the book was originally written as a promotional item to draw attention to the yet-unnamed groups of drunks in New York City and Akron, Ohio. It was simply Bill's attempt to describe his own experience in such a way as to create interest in others.

It took some time for that to materialize, but within a couple of years, it was doing just that. Another, and most likely unexpected, result of the book was that it seemed to codify the many wide and varied thoughts and ideas about what the essentials of the fledgling fellowships were, and as such became the first volume in the canon of Alcoholics Anonymous literature. With his attempt to write an effective promotional volume, he inadvertently published what was quickly seen to be the recipe.

To be fair, I don't think Bill ever intended for the book to become the scripture that it has. For better or worse, however, it almost immediately began to define what it was to be a member of AA; The yardstick with which members could measure themselves, and quite often, each other!

> "The almost unwitting concession by most of the members of the early bands of humans; that someone else was better equipped or more qualified to handle affairs that they themselves felt inadequate to deal with, had to have been the genesis of the evolution of culture itself."

That is an excerpt from another of my essays, "Back to Basics," which helps explain the basic tendency of groups of people to sort themselves almost automatically into a hierarchy.

If early AA is viewed from that perspective, it is easy to imagine what a relief it would have been for many of the early members when Bill published the road map for the "Broad Highway" that he refers to in chapter four.

As the contents of the book were digested, the hopes that new members had that they could find a way to stay sober began to crystallize into the belief that not only was it possible, but also that Bill had defined the method. Unequivocally. As that belief matured, so did the assumption that it needed to be followed without question.

With that in mind, it's not difficult to imagine that the conservative, fundamentalist "all the answers are in the book" group of folks began to emerge early. They were able to very quickly discount the caveats that Bill had included in the book, such as "here are the steps we took which are suggested" *(Alcoholics Anonymous p.59)* and "Our book is meant to be suggestive only. We realize we know only a little." *(Alcoholics Anonymous p.164)*

What is not often talked about is the fact that the final editing of the language of the book creates the illusion that it describes a consensus opinion of the early members. That certainly was not the case. More than a few of the Akron members had not agreed with the need for the book at all, and several of the skeptics in New York lobbied Bill right into the final hours before the initial printing to soften the language of the steps. Bill's declaration that "We have a way out on which we can absolutely agree"*(Alcoholics Anonymous p.17)* is a prime example of his willingness to stretch the truth a bit, but once again (as always, it would seem), with the idea of making the fellowship appear more attractive to prospective members.

Another of the most fundamental aspects of any culture is the tribal instinct that seems to develop quickly. That sense of "us and them" was likely felt more acutely by the early members of AA simply because of the social stigma attached to alcoholism.

The early gatherings were borderline secret societies. The very name adopted by the overall organization continues to reflect that. You would not have to attend too many meetings today before you would hear someone refer to "the normies out *there*."

I imagine that a similar sense of separateness began to evolve rather quickly between the by-the-book folks and others who had their own ideas about the matter.

With that in mind, let's return to the premise of the automatic hierarchy that would suggest a couple of fundamental reasons for there always having been a majority of members who have professed acceptance of the basic beliefs posited by AA.

It would be fair to say that a significant number of those who accepted the basic tenants of AA had no better opinions of their own. But it would be a mistake not to recognize the appeal of that sense of security provided by being on the "us" side of that sense of "us and them."

So, the culture has evolved around adherence to the "program" (code for "by the book"). Even the most casual of observers can identify the basics of Alcoholics Anonymous as the Twelve Steps and a Higher Power. But that observation is too casual.

Alcoholics Anonymous is about much more than whether you follow the dogma of the book religiously, tweak it a little or a lot, or ignore it all together. We can get lost here, if we focus too closely on the doctrinal differences of opinion, and don't step back and recognize that the culture involves much more.

Even though Bill Wilson primarily gets credit for the initial founding of AA, I think his ongoing observations and guidance after the fact are at least as important.

The initial response to the book was disappointing to say the least. It certainly fell short of expectations. It was nearly two years later in March 1941 that an article written by Jack Alexander and published in the *Saturday Evening Post*, at last began to bring some public awareness to the existence of AA.

That article, combined with a series of articles in the *Cleveland Plain Dealer*, resulted in the flood of interest that Bill and the others had expected to come with the initial publication of the book. The growth that ensued did not come without accompanying growing pains, however. As new groups began to establish themselves around the country, there was a never-ending stream of requests to New York for guidance concerning the governance of those groups.

Bill was privy to most of these inquiries and replied personally to as many of them as he could. The details of those many dilemmas are not relevant here other than noting that Bill was increasingly aware of the need to provide some sense of unity and a description of some common ground.

The result of that, and Bill's approach to it, is indeed novel. Rather than offering an opinion on what Alcoholics Anonymous is, and then defining the rules and regulations that needed to be followed in order to be compliant, Bill expounded his opinions with a negative approach. Those opinions first appeared in print in the April 1946 issue of *Grapevine* magazine as "Twelve Points to Assure Our Future." With minimal editing those points came to be known as the long form of the Twelve Traditions. Traditions that say a lot more about what AA isn't than about what it is.

What a contrast!

Bill's authorship of the basic text (a term used fondly by the evangelical members), provides a foundation for the traditional method of reliance on an interventionist deity. However, the *Yang* of "this is how it's done dammit", is complemented nicely by the *Yin* of "there is no wrong way to do the right thing" that he came to realize and expressed in many of his later writings.

I find it much easier to describe my opinions about the birth of the culture of AA, and how it has come to be what it is, than to offer an opinion on exactly what that *is*.

Allow me to paraphrase an opinion from Ernest Kurtz, a noted AA historian, who said, "There really is no such thing as Alcoholics Anonymous. It is a mythos. In reality, what we have are a variety of Alcoholics Anonymous *experiences*."

For some, those experiences are brief and unfulfilling. For others, they are life changing and become life defining.

I offer this from another of my essays entitled "Three Things" as the summation of this one:

> "The essence of what Alcoholics Anonymous is can best be described by what it does. There are no words, no teachings, no ritual, that can

compare with, or describe, the unexpected compassion and empathy that simply flows from one drunk to another."

THE INVISIBLE LINE

The general format of the book Alcoholics Anonymous contains what is now most often referred to as the "first 164," which was written by Bill Wilson (with the exception of the chapter "To Employers" that was penned by Hank Parkhurst).

The remainder of the book has always been devoted to the personal stories of AA members. There were twenty-nine such stories in the first edition, and in each of the subsequent editions some of them remained and others were replaced with new ones. The number also increased—thirty-seven in the second edition, forty-three in the third, and forty-two in the fourth. The primary reason for the changes was to present an up-to-date sense of reality. Keeping a finger on the pulse so to speak.

Early in the summer of 2022, the literature committee of the General Service Office issued an invitation to the general membership of Alcoholics Anonymous to submit their own stories for possible inclusion in the upcoming fifth edition of the book. The following is the piece that I submitted to them in early August of that year.

"ALCOHOL ALLOWED ME TO LIVE with just how far down the toilet my life had really gone, as it continued to allow me to dream about how it was going to be someday."

The significance of that statement has grown over the years. It may not have seemed so profound when I first uttered it nearly two decades ago, but as I have continued to look at my life through that lens, its truth resonates ever more deeply.

Recently I began to reacquaint myself with a friend who I had neither seen nor spoken with for over forty years. In one of my emails to him, as I described what I had been up to all those years, I recounted my adventures as a contractor.

"In 1976 I began a small concrete construction business, and it was quite successful for several years. But for all the skill and knowledge I had in the work that I was doing, I was equally oblivious to overall economics and sound business practices. The runaway inflation and incredible rise in interest rates in the late 70s and into the early 80s caused home building to come screeching to a virtual halt. That was the underlying cause of the failure of the business, but my unwitting ignorance, and my head-in-the-sand optimism that it would bounce back tomorrow, allowed me to sit in the bar day after day, spending money from accounts receivable and ignoring accounts payable while I waited for the day when it would be just like the 'good ole days.' That was the real culprit.

The failure of that business was accompanied by the need to sell a beautiful home that I had built for myself and [my then wife] Janie and move to the inner city. I had intended that move to be temporary, but it was nearly a decade later that I finally gave up the deed to that home in lieu of foreclosure."

As I contemplated my description of those events from 1980, I realized that the effect that alcohol had on me had always been the same. It had been in evidence then, ten years before I had finally gotten sober, and it was the prevalent mindset during the decade that followed, but it had been there from the beginning. This statement may not apply to anyone other than me, but this was my experience:

From the very first drink, alcohol allowed, and often precipitated, the creation of an alternate reality.

Most of the folks who I have heard talk about the invisible line that seems to delineate social drinking from alcoholic drinking, or a normal life from an abnormal one, seem to find it nebulous; they are unable to clearly define the timing of its having been crossed.

That is not my experience. In retrospect it is a simple matter to identify the day I stepped over that line, or perhaps more accurately described, found myself over it without even realizing it. It was November 27, 1969, Thanksgiving Day.

My first wife and I had been invited to share dinner with my family that day, with one strict caveat: dinner was to be at 1:00 p.m. sharp, since my dad had to work a swing shift and had to leave for work at 2:30 p.m. My then wife had little respect for anyone's time other than her own. She was late for virtually everything, and that day was no different. We showed up several minutes late and at the point when everyone else had decided that they could wait for us no longer. They were just beginning to be seated and about the begin their meal when we arrived.

My spouse threw a fit. The ensuing brouhaha was brief however as I promptly escorted her out of the house and drove her home, and then gruffly suggested that she get the hell out of the car. I don't remember having any particular plan as I drove away, but within a few minutes I found myself in the "Blue Note Lounge."

Being only twenty years old, I was not yet familiar with the life of a bar drinker. I only knew of this particular establishment as the result of my having been there a couple of times with the fellows I worked for.

Since I rode to and from work with them, when they stopped for a beer on the way home, I did too.

I have thought about those first few minutes in the Blue Note dozens of times since. I have spoken about it on occasion, most often in meetings, but as I contemplate writing it down, it seems surreal.

It took a couple of minutes for my eyes to adjust to the dim lighting, and as that happened, I took in the aura of the place. Perhaps the first noticeable thing was the aroma—it was not pleasant. Stale cigarette smoke, stale beer. But the *most* noticeable thing about the whole experience were the people who were there. A half dozen or so, all of whom appeared to be old. From my perspective, *really* old. They were all gathered at one end of the bar where the bartender was also seated.

It had been less than thirty minutes since I had left a living room full of loving friends and family, and the overwhelming thought that occurred to me was this: "How sad that these poor folks have nowhere else to be on Thanksgiving Day!"

However, when the bartender threw us all out at 1:00 a.m., some ten or eleven hours later, I had some new best friends!

What I really want to explore here are the subtle changes in my perspective that came about as the result of those few hours in that bar.

I had been drinking "on occasion" for several years prior to that, but most of those occasions were the "fun and games" of teenage drinking. "Let's get drunk and puke and be somebody!" as one friend described it.

As I think back on those events it seems clear that they were an attempt to *temporarily* leave reality (such as it was) and create an alternative. When the hangover subsided, the bell rang for class to begin, or the time clock was punched, it was back to business as usual.

That was the subtle difference; after that experience in the bar, I did not *want* to go back to the reality I had known.

I did not realize it at the time, but from that moment forward all the major decisions in my life were based on the availability and the social acceptability of alcohol. That did not change over the next twenty years. As I look back on it now, I realize that I quite literally stepped out of the culture in which I had been raised, abandoning the social norms affiliated with it, and began to investigate and adopt a completely different sense of reality. Drinking was no longer occasional; it was rapidly becoming an integral component of an entirely new baseline. I had indeed discovered that "sense of ease and comfort" that Dr. Silkworth described, and I had every intention of maintaining that as my default condition. A broader perspective of Dr. Silkworth's comment reveals that that sense of ease and comfort "comes at once as the result of taking a few drinks," and there it is: the alternate reality fueled by alcohol.

My life began to change quickly after that fateful Thanksgiving Day, and in some significant ways. Vikki and I agreed that neither of us wanted to be married, so the separation soon followed. That, coupled with my financial circumstances, required me to move back home with my parents. The prospect of spending my leisure time with them was *so* unattractive, I began to spend a lot of my time at the Blue Note.

Not long after my move home, I had a disagreement with my employer and found myself without a job. While I waited for my promised back wages to be paid, I spent even more time at the bar. My limited funds were dwindling, but I discovered a neat trick—if I took my guitar into the bar and accompanied myself as I sang a couple of tunes, folks would buy me a beer. Or two or three. What a deal!

Another crucial event occurred as I was establishing my residency at the Blue Note. A fellow I knew from growing up in the neighborhood showed up at the bar. I'd admired his skills with a guitar when I was young and here he was in my regular haunt.

He was a few years older than me, and I had not seen him for some time. I soon learned that he had been on the West Coast making a living performing in bars and night clubs, and I was intrigued to say the least. Imagine my surprise and delight when a few weeks later he asked me if I wanted to start a band. My answer required no deliberation and was an emphatic, "Hell yes!"

So we did.

Another noteworthy event from this time: The owner of the Blue Note took me aside one day and pointed out that I was spending a lot of my time there and made this suggestion: "Why don't you tend bar a few days a week? I'll give you ten dollars a shift and within reason you can still drink as much as you want."

How in the world could I turn *that* down?

By the time my twenty-first birthday arrived in May of 1970, I was a completely different person than the one who had walked into that bar just six months earlier. I had gone from a fairly newlywed young man working an entry level job in the construction industry who had at least occasional aspirations of returning to college someday, to one with fanciful dreams of being a professional musician who was playing with what could only be described as a pitiful band, and who was supplementing that meager income tending bar in a stinky-ass beer tavern.

There is no need to detail any of the next few years other than mentioning I had begun a relationship with a woman who was a cocktail waitress in one of the clubs that was a stop in the travels of a couple of later bands. We ultimately settled down and married after I abandoned the notion of a career in the music business, and about the same time as I had begun the aforementioned contracting business.

I don't think that I am much different from most alcoholics in that my drinking had become problematic for others long before it became problematic for me. The first rumblings of my wife's discontent came at about the same time that we moved to the city. We had a daughter barely a year old and we were expecting another child, which no doubt factored into her insistence that I grow up and pay more attention to the reality of our lives. Over a period of time, she had quit drinking altogether, and simply could not comprehend my unwillingness to at least slow down. I could not understand what the big deal was. One of the things that had attracted me to her in the first place was the fact that she drank just like I did.

As the frequency and the intensity of those most uncomfortable discussions increased, she began to reveal details of her youth that she had never mentioned. The most poignant of those revelations was the fact that as a young teen she had watched her mother die from alcoholism. Most unsettling was her pointing out that she was becoming increasingly alarmed by the frightening similarities between my attitudes and behaviors and those of her mother.

She ultimately left in 1985 with these chilling words that I have heard repeated so many times in Alcoholics Anonymous:

> "I love you too much to stand by and watch you killing yourself."

I was not a blackout drinker, but the memory of the last few years of that decade remain pretty gray. There were a couple of relationships, several different jobs, and even a couple of brief forays into the rooms of AA. It was sometime in 1989 that the question that literally changed my life was asked.

One of the most pivotal moments in my life came as the result of that question, and a remarkably simple question it was, "What are your goals?"

My answer, though I didn't verbalize it, was "to get drunk today, and maybe drunker on the weekend."

The question was not nearly as shocking as the answer. The question came as the result of my having sent the woman in my life at the time to Al-Anon. Our relationship had been getting a bit shaky, and both of us sensed that my drinking may have had a little something to do with it. But I was not interested in life without alcohol. As I mentioned earlier, I had some cursory experience with Alcoholics Anonymous in the few years prior and had heard of Al-Anon.

It had occurred to me that they may be able to help her accept living with a drunk like me.

It didn't work out. We soon parted ways, (certainly not my idea), and would see each other only once after that. That occasion was over a year later, and it was meaningful only as it pertained to my making some serious amends.

It certainly was not the question itself that was so unnerving, but rather the sudden realization that I had indeed given up *everything* in order to continue to drink. As I pointed out in my opening statement, I had for many years been able to drink away the increasingly uncomfortable reality of what my life had become, while I continued to live in my own little fantasy world about how my life would be *someday*. In that instant, with that simple question, she had completely shattered that fantasy world. I realized that I had given up even the *illusion* of it being different someday. I also realized in a flash of reality that my life would never *be* any different until I *did* something different.

The dilemma that I lived with over the next few months is described by Bill as "the jumping off place." I could not imagine life with alcohol, nor without it. I was just as miserable when I was drinking as I was when I was not.

There was another critical juncture sometime in 1989 as I attempted to reestablish employment with a company that I had previously burned by packing up my tools and walking off the jobsite in the middle of the day. My motive, although it was only semi-conscious, was that they provided health insurance after a few months of employment, and I was beginning to toy with the notion of looking into a rehab.

There was a slim chance of them having any willingness to hire me, except for the fact that they had recently been awarded a large contract in another city and were looking for tradespeople who were willing to relocate, at least temporarily. "Oh, I'm your guy!" I assured them.

In the spring of the following year, I *did* find myself in a spin-dry facility, and was a little dismayed with what I found. I'm not sure what my expectations actually were, maybe a magic wand or some of Cheech and Chong's magic dust, but what I soon realized was that I was being reintroduced to Alcoholics Anonymous. I sometimes jokingly suggest that the cost of my first *Big Book* was my $14,000 co-pay.

The insurance proved to be inadequate, and my stay was short, but it was a start. However, after just a few weeks of sobriety I was drinking again. I have very little recollection of the couple of weeks that followed, but I recall vividly the knocking on the door of the apartment early on a Friday morning. As I begrudgingly opened my eyes and looked around, I realized that I had been napping on the living room floor, again, and was cuddled up with an empty vodka bottle. Again.

I was shocked and dismayed to see my mother and dad standing on the porch when I finally answered the door. My only thought was, "Oh my God, I must have invited them to visit." Since I was sober, or so I assumed that's what they thought, I reluctantly allowed them to whisk me off to their fifth-wheel trailer, which was parked at one of the RV campgrounds on the outskirts of town.

Without profanity it is nearly impossible to describe the anguish and the trauma of the time spent cloistered in that travel trailer. I have since described it as my having been kidnapped and held hostage for the day. The desire and the physical need for a drink were almost unbearable. And all the while my mother was cheerfully rambling on about what seemed to be the most ridiculous of things: Aunt Millie and Uncle Ralph, and all the guys from my high school days that she still ran into on occasion and her asking why didn't I get in touch with some of them.

As the afternoon wore on, however, another pivotal bombshell question was posed. This time asked by my mother, a question and its answer that literally changed the trajectory of my life.

"What do you want to do this evening?"

From seemingly out of nowhere came my reply, "I think there is a speaker meeting at the Triangle Club, would you like to go to that?"

We did.

I haven't had a drink since.

The significance of that whole experience is this: the thought of not drinking that day would never have crossed my mind had my parents not interfered. However, twenty-four hours later, since I had already suffered the consequences of not drinking that first day, I found the willingness and resolve to suffer the consequences of not drinking on the second day and scurried off to a morning meeting rather than to another bottle of vodka.

I acquired a sponsor within the next few days, who turned out to be more of a friend than any kind of mentor, but whose friendship was still invaluable at the time. Undoubtedly more influential in the first few weeks and months of my sobriety, however, was the relationship that was quickly developing with a retired couple, particularly the woman, who seemed determined to tuck me under her wing and shoo me along with her wherever she went. In retrospect I can only describe the two of them as having been completely caught up in the vortex that is the busy-ness of AA.

Consequently, I too became very busy in AA. I don't regret a minute of it. I received a crash course in a wide array of some of the less glamorous aspects of AA that I may never have experienced otherwise. I would not have volunteered for many of the things that this couple had me participating in.

On the first anniversary of that Friday morning knock on my door, I realized that I was not really very excited with the prospect of celebrating a year of sobriety in the fashion that was the tradition of the group in which I found myself that day.

There were balloons and cakes, and all manner of back-slapping, accompanied by the wide assortment of obligatory comments ranging from "I knew you could do it" to "I'd a lost money on that one."

The realization that I was expected to sit at the table facing the rest of the room, and lead the meeting, was very unsettling.

I did it, of course. But when I shared, the message that I tried so desperately to convey was that the celebration that I was experiencing was not that of marching bands and parades, but one of stillness. A stillness that was the exact antithesis of the quiet desperation that had defined my life for so long—the desperation that I had come to accept would last forever.

I did not recognize it at the time, but over the years that stillness has become some sort of divine ground for me. In fact, for most of those years I have described my path as having been nothing more complicated than learning to be still.

There would certainly seem to be a dichotomy between the busy-ness that I described earlier, and the stillness that I have just alluded to. One of the things that I have been pointing out for a good many years is the fact that in my mind there is a distinct difference between getting sober, staying sober, and simply being sober. I don't find it difficult to see the correlation between getting and staying sober and all the effort that is expended in the busy-ness of doing that, nor do I see any difference between being still and simply being sober.

Primarily because of my very early exposure to "Big Book study meetings" and "Twelve and Twelve study groups", I suppose you could say that my initial foray into and through the process of the steps was "by the book." It has only been through the years that have followed that I have had the time and opportunity to question and contemplate the true essence of the steps and my participation in the process that I have begun to understand and appreciate the significance of it all.

That questioning and pondering has led me to some simple yet very profound truths.

One of the first things I realized was that I had known since childhood how to behave; that I had never had any need for the legislated moralities of either religions or governments. However, along with that realization came the recognition of just how frequently I had simply ignored that sense of integrity over the previous twenty-some years.

The process of the steps has provided a reconciliation between the stories that I had been telling myself about the past and the reality of the present—even more important was the reconnection with that sense of integrity. But most importantly I realized that it was incumbent upon me to pay attention moving forward so as to avoid compromising that intuitive wisdom.

That paying of attention has turned out to be my understanding of the tenth step. It is my opinion that the tenth step is nothing *more* than paying attention.

Another of those fundamental truths, and possibly the most profound, was the realization that everything I have ever been told or read, regardless of the source, is merely someone's opinion.

The letting go of old ideas has been a years long process that will undoubtedly continue for as long as I am capable of *having* ideas. There is no need to probe the delight of that journey here; what *is* vitally important however is how that applies to how I think about my thinking.

Questioning old ideas is one thing, being willing to question your very thoughts is quite another. When I am paying attention however, (step ten) I can see just how little most of my thinking actually pertains to any sort of reality. The eleventh step is a vital part of discounting the fantasy worlds of both past and future, and the beginning of paying attention (ten again) to the eternal present. When thoughts that are questioned are deemed to be false, they seem to simply dissipate on their own. This process is about allowing the mind to quiet itself and experience the stillness that I have been pointing to.

The fusion of these two simple concepts, the critical awareness of ten, and the results of allowing my thinking to quiet itself and recognize the stillness through eleven, is what many seekers refer to as mindfulness.

However, mindfulness as a noun is just a word; it is only when the adverb mindfully begins to describe my everyday thoughts and actions that its value is realized.

I have been cautious as I have described my journey here. The spiritual awareness that has come as the result of this entire process and my spiritual practice as an agnostic that has evolved out of that are both way beyond the confines of traditional Alcoholics Anonymous.

That said, please allow me to point out that I recognized many years ago that AA is how I can make a difference. I continue to participate, and cannot imagine ever not participating. Which points directly to this statement that I make with some regularity: Alcoholics Anonymous has not changed my life, but my participation in it absolutely has.

THE GRAND EXPERIENCE

OVER THE YEARS MUCH HAS been made of the "spiritual experience" that Bill Wilson noted as the turning point in his life. It had occurred in December of 1934 in Town's Hospital in New York City. In fact, I have written elsewhere that I consider that experience to be the first chapter in the origin story of Alcoholics Anonymous.

Until now, however, nothing has *ever* been made of what I consider to be a similar experience of mine on the South Rim of the Grand Canyon in 2000. Until now it has never been written about, nor has it even been discussed much.

I have no idea what actually occurred in New York in 1934, I wasn't there. And I am chuckling as I write this: I have no idea what actually transpired in Arizona in 2000 either, and I *was* there!

I recall having read this opinion somewhere: "All experiences, even the most profound and deeply felt spiritual experiences, come to pass, never to stay." What then you may be tempted to ask, is the big deal about these so-called spiritual experiences?

It seems to be the effect or the results of those experiences that have the potential of making a difference. It is a shift in consciousness, or more simply a change in perspective, that can quite literally change the course of one's life.

I have spent a great deal of time and effort researching and attempting to understand Bill's experience and its effects, but hardly any time at all considering my own. I suspect my understanding of Bill's experience, or at least my opinion of it, will be of value as it pertains to examining my experience.

In order to move on, let me get straight to my opinion of what Bill almost off-handedly referred to in the second appendix of the book *Alcoholics Anonymous* as a "sudden and spectacular upheaval."

There is ample evidence that would suggest that Bill may have been hallucinating at the time he was experiencing "the great clean wind of a mountain top blowing through and through." *(Alcoholics Anonymous p. 13)*

The most commonly administered treatment for alcoholics at Towns Hospital was known as the belladonna cure, which was known to cause hallucinations; hallucinations which were in fact anticipated. The actual details of the experience itself, which have been described by Bill in various ways in subsequent telling's, are not nearly as important as the results.

As a minimum of historical background, it must be pointed out that as the result of his inability to not drink, Bill was very nearly at the end. His wife Lois had been forewarned that permanent hospitalization or residency at a sanitarium was quite likely in his future.

But then seemingly out of nowhere Bill's longtime friend Ebby Thatcher unexpectedly showed up sober, and insisted that his adoption of the evangelical message of the Oxford Group was the reason that he was no longer drinking. Bill was surely hanging on to the possibility of that being his salvation as well as he entered Towns for the fourth time early that winter.

My point is this: Bill was primed to interpret the events of that experience the way that he did. It would not have been much of a stretch for him to reach the conclusion that he did, and later described this way: "This must be the great reality, the God of the preachers." *(Pass It On p. 121)*

Now for some background for the other side of this story. In the early 1970s I spent several years pursuing a career as a musician. In 2021 I ran into a friend who I had not seen in years; we began reacquainting ourselves via email. That friend was the bass player in several of the bands that I had worked with. This is a conversation from one of those emails.

A question from him: "Are you still strumming and singing?"

My reply: A very simple and straight forward question to be sure. The answer however is much more complicated, but in a word, no.

The details of the chronology escape me now, but sometime around '73–'74, I was in Pocatello, living with Janie. I was working a construction job in the daytime and playing bass for Mike Spears in the evening. I don't know for sure when it happened, and I don't think it was sudden, but I began to realize that I was not nearly as talented as I had always thought I was.

As the result of that and the desire to stay connected in some way with the music, I began to buy sound equipment—PA, mics, mixing board, etc.—and began the attempt to produce a successful band rather than play in one.

I think it was in late 1974 that Mike and I were at a Wishbone Ash concert in the old Terrace Ballroom in SLC. I'm sure that I was high on the psychedelic de jour, and that may have enhanced this experience considerably, but an incredible thing happened that evening.

At some point in the show the members of the band began to make fun of Salt Lake City, and then the LDS church and their missionaries that they had seen in the UK. Before long they were literally spitting on the fans in the first few rows. And the crowd was cheering them on!

I suddenly realized the brute force of the power that these entertainers had over the crowd. To be blunt, it frightened me.

You may or may not recall, but Mike was absolutely obsessed with making it to "the big stage," his description of success. And I was presumably along for the ride. At that point I had to ask myself whether I would be capable of using that power wisely if and when I ever had the opportunity. My answer was that I did not know, but more importantly I realized that I was unwilling to take the chance of *not* being capable.

Before that night was over, I had sold my equipment to Mike (which he never paid for) and walked away.

Not long afterward I had convinced Janie to move to Salt Lake with me, and had begun in earnest to develop a career in the building trades, most specifically as a carpenter.

At some point during the next couple of years I had a whimsical notion that playing a steel guitar would be a neat trick, so I bought one. An expensive one. Much to my dismay I discovered that learning to play a steel guitar is a daunting task. It was not long before my interest waned, and that guitar was added to the long list of guitars that I would eventually leave in pawn shops as my drinking worsened.

That email describes the turning of a page. Over the next few months Janie and I decided that we would *probably* settle down, *probably* get married, *probably* start a family, and that I would *probably* start a business.

But we also decided that before we committed ourselves to playing by most of the rules, we should take the road trip of a lifetime. And it would *probably* have to be then or never. That's exactly what we did, embarking on a journey lasting just over three months that was a most delightful adventure. The aspect of that trip that pertains to this story, however, is simply this: it began at the Grand Canyon.

My late wife Gail and I had been together for several years before I discovered that even though she had spent most of her life in Las Vegas, she had never been to the Grand Canyon, which is just a few hours away. I had many fond memories from the ten days or so that I had spent there years before and began to insist that we visit soon. (Gail was not much of a nature person. Her idea of roughing it was no room service after 10:00 p.m.)

She finally agreed, however, and I booked a package deal that included a day trip to the canyon via the steam railroad—which was originally the only means of access other than on foot or horseback—bookended by two nights in Williams, the point of departure for the train. A shuttle bus provided transportation between the various lookout points on the rim itself.

Within the first few minutes of the few hours that we had on the rim, Gail set the tone. When we managed to make our way through the crowd to the railing at the first stop, she looked around for a few seconds and then said, "That's nice, where's the gift shop?"

The rest of the day can be described with one word: touristy.

All that lingers in my memory of the next few hours now is the crowd, the noise, the all-too-frequent reminders to move along in order to stay on schedule and being generally distracted from the canyon itself. As the afternoon ended however, we were back near the train stop, away from most of the crowds, and had a few moments to just sit and enjoy the canyon. Gail quickly grew tired of the sitting and went off, to find another gift shop I suppose; at any rate she left me alone. Just me. With the magnificence that is the Grand Canyon.

The description that follows is tricky because I'm not sure if I am describing what actually happened, or if I am describing my attempts to explain to *myself* what happened. Either way this is what I recall. The first thing that came to mind as I sat there were the fond memories from twenty-five years earlier of having been there as a twenty-six-year-old man with a vast array of hopes and dreams, goals and ambitions, and an incredible amount of optimism. The world by the tail so to speak. But as I sat, I experienced the euphoria of all that begin to crumble. As if in a stop-action film, with increasing speed I witnessed the next fifteen years of my life melt into the pool of despair that is active alcoholism. Suddenly it stopped. In what I can only describe as a rebirth, I found myself in Alcoholics Anonymous again and paying attention. Learning to trust the process and being amazed that I could live without alcohol. The rest of my experience that afternoon was reliving the first ten years of my sobriety, and the incredible gratitude of simply being right there at that moment.

When I rejoined my wife a few minutes later, she had a startled look on her face. She looked at me and immediately asked, "Are you OK?" The only response that I could offer was, "Yes, but I can't begin to tell you how OK I am."

I could hardly speak for the next couple of hours; it was several weeks before I could talk about the experience at all.

Are there any similarities between these two seemingly widely different experiences? Perhaps not so much between these two in particular, but I think there are commonalities with all such events.

I have described my experience as having been "out of body," or perhaps more accurately stated "out of mind." I think that may be key. These events seem to occur beyond the mind's ability to think and process. But the egoic construct of the mind quickly attempts to intercede and make sense of what appears to be *non*-sensical and unsettling. The eventual effect of the experience is influenced deeply by the state of mind prior to its occurrence.

I think that points clearly to the differences between the two experiences that I have described.

Bill was searching desperately for something that could relieve him of his alcoholism. So that was most certainly on his mind. His recent exposure to the fundamentalist Christian doctrine of the Oxford Group raised his expectations of that doctrine being the solution. The result or effect of his experience was almost foreseeable: he immediately embraced the theology of Western religion as it was viewed by most of the members of the culture of the time, and viewed that as having been the cause of his miraculously having lost the desire to drink. In his mind, the two seemed inextricably linked. He was looking for answers and he found some.

In 2000, I had been sober for ten years, married for all but two of them, been gainfully employed through the Carpenters Union, and a homeowner for most of those years. Unlike the circumstances of Bill's life in 1934, or my life in 1990 for that matter, my life in 2000 was not in critical condition.

Surprisingly, after the initial jostling of my consciousness, the memory of the event at the Grand Canyon began to fade quickly. In fact, I now realize that before I had begun to contemplate it in order to write this piece, I have rarely thought of it at all in recent years. So what was the effect of that? If the effect was minimal, or short lived, what was the point of it at all?

I had been sober no more than a couple of years before I began to question the validity of what seemed to be a very rigid and dogmatic approach to the methods and procedures of traditional AA. I was far too timid to verbalize those opinions, however. As time went on my opinions grew stronger, but I remained hesitant to discuss them with anyone, and I was certainly unwilling to bring the topic up in public.

What I realize now is that the effect of my experience at the grandest of all canyons was simply this: a very subtle yet powerful message of confirmation.

That the path I was on, and continue to travel, was and is valid.

Bill got answers. I realized the legitimacy of questions.

THREE THINGS

OVER THE YEARS THAT I have been sober, I have acquired a wonderful trust and a deep faith in Alcoholics Anonymous. But that has not come without some investigation into, and the understanding of, several different facets of it.

One of the most prevalent misconceptions that I have seen and heard over the years is that Bill Wilson personally had, or that AA in general has, all the answers. Bill wrote several disclaimers addressing that in the *Big Book*, but not everyone has noticed.

For this discussion I have identified three separate aspects of AA that deserve more than just casual consideration. The first would certainly have to be the disease concept of alcoholism. Equally important and at least as misunderstood, is the question as to whether AA is fundamentally religious. Some simple research into the history of AA in general, and these two topics in particular, is the third element, and it is that which ties this all together. A word of caution here; by research I do not mean taking at face value, and most certainly not accepting as the truth, all that you hear in meetings.

Dr. Silkworth was certainly not the first in the medical community to suspect strongly that alcoholism, especially as it manifests in later stages, had some biological and physiological component. However, it was the ensuing success (though modest in the beginning) of AA and his link to its origins, that brought his opinions into the more generally accepted theories about the nature of alcoholism.

However as was the case in the early days of AA, I will mark that concept as duly noted and set it aside for now.

God and religion have long been seen as the solution to *all* the ills of society. The drunken misbehavior of some of its citizens is generally seen as one of the more egregious sins that could and should be resolved with some repentance and piety.

Without any intent to discount anyone else's opinion of Bill's experience in Towns Hospital, mine is that the effect of that experience was Bill's having gotten off the fence and having returned to the religious admonitions from his past. And that's what he began to preach.

It is well documented that evangelical Bill was totally ineffective. Dr. Silkworth chided him and suggested that he stop trying to convert his prospects.

But after some modicum of success with Dr. Bob and those who followed, Bill's religious approach began to build some credibility. Not necessarily with the public in general, but most certainly with the new prospects who could see other drunks whose stories were so similar to their own, but were no longer drinking.

Bill occasionally referred to the early members as "last gaspers," or more commonly, as "low-bottom drunks." He included himself in that lot. He described the despair and hopelessness of that in many of his writings. The reason I make note of it is this: they all seemed to be "willing to go to any length", and since the religious doctrine of the Oxford Group is what was on the table, they submitted to that.

One can only imagine what the mindset of those early members really was. Had all of them really been persuaded that the solution (which was being sold as a "spiritual rather than religious" one) was what was keeping them sober? Or were there some, as there are today, that went along with the rest simply because they were afraid not to?

The point that I want to make here is this: Regardless of the reason or reasons these folks were staying sober, the solution was being sold as a belief in some concept of God. As many of the earliest members stayed sober, and the number of new members grew, there seemed to be mounting evidence that the application of this time-honored theology was the answer. Hence this bit of deductive reasoning didn't seem to be misguided at all: Spiritual solution? Must be a spiritual malady.

There were several early members who were more than a little skeptical of the religious point of view however. Perhaps the most noteworthy of them was Jim Burwell. Not only did he steadfastly refuse to acknowledge any belief in God, he was also very insistent that the fledgling fellowship not be so adamant about that being a requirement. And much to the consternation of the more pious members, he was staying sober.

Even as the final editing of the *Alcoholics Anonymous* manuscript was nearing completion, the heated discussions about the actual wording of the steps continued. The significant compromises that Bill finally agreed to were the addition of *"As we understood Him"* in steps three and eleven, and the elimination of *"on your knees"* in step seven.

Although the descriptive language of the early literature was softened a bit, the practical application of the steps and most of the other aspects of AA remained firmly entrenched in the theological traditions of the West.

How quickly they had begun to ignore Silky's hypothesis that alcoholism is a physiological and biological disorder and not a moral issue.

I am not qualified to speak from a medical or controlled research point of view, nor am I particularly interested in the finer details of those studies. What does hold great interest for me however is the overwhelming evidence that alcoholism is a physiological disease, which exists with or without alcohol. Other details such as genetic predisposition and ethnic tendencies are not overwhelmingly important here.

What *is* vitally important however, is to understand that the disease of alcoholism is *not* caused by any of the usual suspects. It is not a moral issue, and by the time the middle stages are reached it is way beyond the matter of choice. It is not caused by social environment, nor psychological or mental issues. The body of an alcoholic lacks the ability to assimilate alcohol in a normal way. So as soon as alcohol is introduced, the alcoholic's body begins to make physical adjustments in order to compensate for that. As *soon as*. We often speak about it being the first drink that gets us drunk. Little did we suspect that in an alcoholic's case it is the *very* first one. The alcoholic becomes addicted to alcohol long before he or anyone else is aware of it simply because the socially unacceptable effects don't begin to show up for a long time. Usually years.

The disease of alcoholism and the dilemma of being human are two separate issues. The only treatment for alcoholism is 100 percent abstinence, but without the alcohol, the human dilemma becomes even more overwhelming. The traditional AA method has been to treat it *all* as alcoholism, ignoring those differences altogether.

The unfortunate reality of all that is this: we have swept up all of the circumstances of an alcoholic's life into one big bundle and labeled the whole ugly mess as the disease of alcoholism. That simply isn't true.

One of the most important aspects of the whole recovery process is the acceptance of the responsibility for past actions and inactions. If you consciously or even unconsciously include those circumstances as being "alcoholism," you have pled guilty to the charge of being an alcoholic! It's not your fault!

We are absolutely responsible for cleaning up the residual effects of our adventures and misadventures, but letting go of the guilt and shame of having done all those things is an essential part of that process. That self-absolution becomes much easier when you recognize that regardless of what you did or didn't do, there was seldom any malicious intent, nor was there a complete lack of morals— it was the fact that your body absolutely demanded more alcohol. No matter what the cost.

Without a clear understanding of that it is easy to remain stuck, agreeing with society's less-than-kind opinion of alcoholics. Unfortunately, traditional AA does little to dispel that. By the time Bill wrote the *Twelve and Twelve*, he seemed to have forgotten completely the opinion of Dr. Silkworth that alcoholism is a physiological disease; he was intent on furthering a moral solution to what was never a moral issue.

Without any way of knowing otherwise, I can only give Bill the benefit of the doubt and assume that it was never his intent to offer any of his writings as being anything more than his opinion, but many of those who have followed since have turned a lot of them into scriptural reference books. That is most unfortunate.

The essence of what Alcoholics Anonymous is can best be described by what it does. There are no words, no teachings, no ritual, that can compare with, or describe, the unexpected compassion and empathy that simply flows from one drunk to another.

Alcoholics Anonymous will not change your life. *You* will change your life. But Alcoholics Anonymous can provide you with a safe place to be, friendships the likes of which you never dreamed possible, and some simple guidelines to follow as you begin the incredible adventure of discovering who you really are.

There is a solution. But it need not be confined to the narrow-minded dogma of your grandfather's AA. I am not advocating any sort of a revolution here. AA is exactly what AA needs to be—right here, right now. But it is incumbent upon each of us to discern what that is for ourselves, and hopefully guide the new folks out of the shadows of the archives and into the light of a more comfortable recovery.

MY DISEASE

> *"The Judeo-Christian universe is one in which the moral urgency, and the anxiety to get it right, pervade everything."* —*Alan Watts*

EVEN THOUGH THE SENSE OR feeling that Watts describes emanates from the theological traditions, it goes deeper than that. We can argue belief vs. non-belief, Spiritual vs. Religious, or East vs. West, endlessly, but the core issue remains.

There seems to be an unspoken, yet ominous, awareness that you are somehow obliged to participate in the titanic battle that purportedly rages endlessly between the forces of good and evil. Even more distressing is the sense that if you're not making the constant effort to fight on the side of righteousness, you have succumbed to the forces of evil, and are, therefore, by default, aligned with the dark side. You are probably evil yourself. "I don't wanna play" is never an acceptable option. Traditional AA thinking does more to perpetuate that sense of dis-ease than to dispel it.

The genesis for the misconception of what constitutes the disease of alcoholism is in the first half of the first step: "We admitted we were powerless over alcohol." That simple statement invokes the perception of some reprehensible supernatural boogeyman with whom we are engaged in constant battle. Scattered throughout the literature are plenty of references that not only support that notion, many of them amplify it further. Cunning, baffling, powerful! Yikes! Scary stuff.

By not recognizing the difference between the disease and the often-devastating effects that come as the result of the excessive drinking that the disease demands, many members of AA have acquired an incredible number of very curious ideas about what alcoholism is.

It seems to be a natural human tendency to deny responsibility for the uncomfortable circumstances of our lives. We are quick to embrace anything on which to lay the blame for the disasters that most of our lives have become. Enter: "My Disease." We now have the perfect scapegoat for anything and everything in our lives. Past, present, even the future.

I have a fond memory of a television commercial from a few years ago in which the sales pitch was for the latest smart phone. It showed a young girl maybe five or six years old, standing on her bed with the phone held high. In the room with her was the monster, presumably from under the bed, with a most perplexed look on his face. The young girl's attention panned back and forth between the Google results displayed on the phone and the perceived threat. Finally, with a burst of confidence she said to him, "This says you're not real!"

It would be interesting to zoom in on all the barely noticeable name tags that adorn the phantom monster's chest. One that would have special interest for me could have come from the pen of Bill Wilson himself who identifies him as "King Alcohol"*(Alcoholics Anonymous p. 151)* and reminds us that he is a "subtle foe."*(Alcoholics Anonymous p. 85)* More contemporary labels would be "my disease," "alcohol-ISM," "the ego," or "my mind."

Bill was persistent with this erroneous personification and subsequent description of alcohol and the disease of alcoholism in those terms. "Cunning, baffling, powerful!" surely paints a frightful picture, but not a particularly accurate one. Even the first step, the very basis of the recovery process, misidentifies the problem; I am *not* powerless over alcohol at all, but I am *absolutely* powerless over what happens in my body when I ingest it.

We are told that honesty is essential, and that honesty with ourselves is the pinnacle of said honesty. But when in meeting after meeting, we hear other members consistently blaming the most ludicrous of behaviors and attitudes on my disease and alcohol-ISM, it becomes tempting to follow suit. We naturally welcome the opportunity to shift any of the blame away from ourselves. When we feel like we're joining the crowd by doing so, it is that much easier.

If this attitude and unwillingness to look at oneself were confined primarily to newer members, it might be dismissed more easily. But I often hear folks with decades of sobriety spouting the same rhetoric.

A large portion of this incongruity seems to stem directly from the nearly total misunderstanding of the physical aspect of the disease of alcoholism. We have been indoctrinated from our inauguration into the program that alcoholism is a physical, mental, and spiritual disease, but there seems to be undue emphasis on the latter two, and an almost flippant dismissal of the first.

So, what about these different aspects of the disease? There is absolutely no denying the horrific mental and emotional anguish, the often-tragic physical circumstances of our lives, and the utter hopelessness that most of us have experienced in the last days of drinking. But for nearly all of us, those things are the *effects* of alcoholism, the horrendous consequences of the insane drinking that the physical disease demands.

Bill does a wonderful job of describing the "jumping-off place" in several places in the book; there is no need to repeat any of that here. What I find interesting however, is the difference in the perception of that nightmare when seen from differing points of view.

When seen from the perspective of the "spiritual angle", it is muddled terribly by our tendency to accept the perception of the immorality, sinfulness, selfishness, and total disregard of anything decent that has always been society's view of the alcoholic. In short: the downright shamefulness of it all.

Unfortunately, that seems to have always been the traditional AA point of view. Bill preaches repeatedly from that pulpit in *Twelve Steps and Twelve Traditions*. The judgment and the conviction are handed down in the very first paragraph of the first chapter:

"It is truly awful to admit that glass in hand, we have warped our minds into such an obsession for destructive drinking that only an act of Providence can remove it from us."

Guilty! (Gavel banging)

Most of us had been reading and rereading that indictment to ourselves for years. "I know this is all my fault." And now the verdict's in, spelled out in black and white, and directly from the expert's mouth.

But what if, on the other hand, we look at that mental obsession and inability to not drink with the awareness of the physical aspects of this disease? Dr. Silkworth presented that opinion from the beginning, but then as now, it was noted and then for the most part ignored.

In the latter stages of this disease the primary reason for an alcoholic's drinking stems from the fact that he is addicted to alcohol. Alcoholism is a physical disease. If you have the physical abnormality that prevents your body from processing ethyl alcohol in ways that are considered normal, you are considered to be an alcoholic. The condition exists regardless of whether or not you drink. If you do drink however, your body must immediately begin to compensate for its inability to process alcohol normally, and these abnormal physical compensations ultimately lead to an addiction to the alcohol. The addiction usually begins quickly, and most often goes unnoticed for a long while.

The thinking of a drinking alcoholic is as far beyond his control as is his ability to not drink. After years of drinking, the alcoholic's body absolutely *needs* alcohol to function. The obsession that seems to consume him, is with the couple of drinks that will get him back to feeling normal. But that first one inevitably begins the nightmare all over again. To suggest that he has had any choice in the matter is absurd. (Unless of course your point of view is still clouded by the notion that this is a moral issue, and that enough repentance and piety will take care of the dilemma once and for all.)

Bill identifies the first step in recovery on page 30. *(Alcoholics Anonymous)* "We learned that we had to fully concede to our innermost selves that we were alcoholic." The significance of that statement is seldom investigated or even talked about. If that concession is in fact "full," then the accompanying surrender is also. This goes much deeper than "admitting," and even beyond accepting. I think a sense of agreement most accurately describes that surrender. This agreement is very matter of fact, without any emotional or intellectual deliberation. There has been neither bargaining, nor negotiation; and it is not a compromise. There is no anger, no self-pity, nor is there resentment toward those who *can* drink. It is simply the awareness that what is *is*.

It seems to me that that agreement is more easily reached when it is seen through the perspective of the disease concept. Without the overtones of immorality and sinfulness, it becomes much easier to go beyond the shame and humiliation of never having measured up, and that dreadful sense of unworthiness, which in and of themselves were reason enough to drink.

The significance of this difference in perspective is monumental. I certainly wouldn't be so bold as to suggest that the process of the steps is any easier, but without the apprehension and fear that you aren't doing them correctly, or quickly enough, and the gnawing anxiety that you may never experience this awakening that everyone is talking about, it seems that the process almost unfolds by itself.

This surrender, or sense of agreement, is not an event, but is more a shift in consciousness. In a very real sense, it *is* that psychic change. To come into agreement with being an alcoholic and looking honestly at what that means, is to also come into agreement with taking the steps necessary to literally alter the course of your life.

When seen from this viewpoint, alcoholism is no longer the enemy, nor is it an excuse. It can simply be accepted as the disease that it is and recognized as the explanation for the insanity that our lives had become. So, this "Spiritual Awakening" is not some mysterious mystical future event to be placed up on a shelf with all the other things that will hopefully make your life comfortable someday. The *experience,* call it spiritual if you like, begins with that concession, and the willingness to come into agreement with life. All of life.

THE RELIGION OF AA

ANY WOULD-BE ENTREPRENEUR IS LIKELY to follow some established models for success. The fundamentals of those models are generally straightforward; the idea is to create a product or a service, and then create the need for that product and/or service. The most successful of those models perpetuate the need by introducing new and improved versions of the product and/or instilling in the consumer the idea that they can never have enough of it.

The religions of the world use that model. The product? Eternal life, a seat in the presence of God, and forgiveness of all your sins. The need? A perpetual reminder that you are forever unworthy and always on the wrong side in the Great Conflict between good and evil.

Is there a price? Of course. There is the path and explicit instruction regarding the following of the path. As well as the stern admonition that anything contrary to following *the* path is a sin, and that even being unaware of the path is a sin.

Conclusion:
- You are a hopeless sinner.
- Only God can save you.

- Only we have the true and infallible way to Him.

See how easy that was?

The religion of AA has replaced the original sin of Western theology with the dreadful sin of alcoholism. The promise of salvation and eternal life is replaced with the promise of sobriety, and the punishment of an everlasting hell is supplanted by the threat of a return to the horror of a drunken nightmare.

Even though Dr. Silkworth postulated that alcoholism is a disease, at the time there had been little research into that theory. Even if you have the inclination to accept the disease concept, without looking into it a little more thoroughly, it remains easy to be seduced by the doctrine of AA into the illusion that you drank your way into alcoholism, and that it is your fault.

It seems that being an alcoholic isn't your fault, but all those nasty things that you did along the way to ultimately become one certainly are. It simply has to be that way for the religious model to work.

With no intent to diminish the importance, nor the validity of, Bill's experience in Towns Hospital, the effect of it was his return to the religious traditions with which he was familiar. His association with the Oxford Group, first in New York through Ebby, and a few months later in Akron with Dr. Bob, solidified that.

Even though the *language* of the *Big Book* was softened somewhat to placate some of the early members whose free thinking was outside the traditional box, the moralist point of view that *defines* the theology of Western civilization remained intact.

By the time the *Twelve and Twelve* was published, the character defects had morphed into deadly sins. The notion of faith in the power of the group being a viable Higher Power was seen as a conciliatory pat on the head for the new folks, who if they had been diligent enough and done everything correctly would have "come to know God and call Him by name!" (Bill's words, not mine.)

No one can possibly know what state of awareness, or the level of serenity that Bill was able to enjoy. All we have as his legacy are his writings, and he himself said that the words in the Big Book and the Twelve and Twelve had "become frozen in time; almost dogmatic."

So, my conclusion is this: If you follow the dogma of Alcoholics Anonymous religiously, it has become just another religion. Not that there is anything inherently wrong with that. In fact, for a lot of folks, there is great comfort in that concept.

But please don't insult my intelligence and sensibility with the worn-out insistence that that can be defined as "spiritual, and not religious."

RELIGION?

I HAD ONCE INTENDED TO use a quote from Carl Jung to bolster an opinion that I was writing about, but I was not sure that I remembered it accurately, so I looked it up to be sure. This is it:

> "One of the main functions of organized religion is to protect people against a direct experience of God."

What was absent from my memory was the word *function*. I immediately thought of this: my opinion about the religion of Alcoholic Anonymous: "If you follow the dogma of Alcoholics Anonymous religiously, Alcoholics Anonymous has become just another religion."

That assertion has ruffled a lot of feathers among AA traditionalists, but as I considered the word "function," I realized that I had missed a key element. AA in and of itself may or may not qualify as a religion, but the culture that has evolved along with it undoubtedly allows it to *function* as one.

There are certainly those who *treat* AA as a religion. When viewed from a theological perspective, the process laid out in the book *Alcoholics Anonymous* closely follows the same model that supports the Abrahamic religions.

So what exactly *is* the function of religion? And what does that have to do with the traditional views of Alcoholics Anonymous?

This investigation should rightly begin several centuries ago with the origin of the word religion itself, as well as the sense or essence that it conveys, rather than limiting ourselves to the modern clinical definition.

Consider this opinion from Bruce Lincoln, a professor of the histories of religions at the University of Chicago.

"If philologists are right to follow Servius in deriving the Latin abstract noun religio from the verb re-ligare, it conveys most fundamentally the sense of reconnecting things, beings, and spheres of existence that once were close but somehow have come to be distant. Understood in this fashion, religion does not just involve, but actually grows out of and responds to a persistent and a poignant sense of ontological separation, alienation, or estrangement. For if this were not actually felt, or if it could ever be fully and conclusively overcome, then the need for religion—for reconnecting that which has been sundered—would in that same millennial moment disappear, just as surely as it would disappear if one could ever accept this sense of estrangement as something that is final and irrevocable, beyond redemption or alteration. Religion thus flourishes in the in-between world that we all inhabit, where the sense of alienation is part of the existential state, but something which may still be overcome—occasionally, partially, and temporarily—in moments of mystic reverie, ecstatic flight, or communal celebration."

That description clearly points to the human dilemma and suggests that religion can be the solution to that dilemma. Lincoln identifies in his concluding sentence the essence of the quest of spiritual aspirants of all disciplines: the seeking. He also quite succinctly points out the disturbing downside of the seeking: the results are "occasional, partial, and temporary." With that simple description, he identifies the genesis of the evolution of religion.

It is interesting to note that Lincoln makes no mention of any metaphysical theory or any supernatural deity in his brief description of religion. However, it is the adoption of one or both of those notions as the solution to the dilemma that creates the necessity of organization.

The origin stories of the earliest cultures were surely based on myths that contained an abundance of both those concepts. The reasoning behind that of course is that the supernatural could explain things that had no other explanations. The underlying fear that was at the core of the sense of separateness was soon allayed by the hope that the future promised by the creators of various paths and methods were valid. As those hopes became more and more fervent, they gradually morphed into beliefs.

As groups of people increase in size, it is inevitable that the need for some sort of organization and governance does too. In the case of early religions, I suspect that the originators of the various beliefs and practices were quick to establish control over both the ideology and the methodology of the groups of seekers, and those groups gradually evolved into *organized* religions.

The appeal of following someone else's lead is obvious, especially if that lead offers answers to the most fundamental of life's questions. Early religious leaders most surely took advantage of that.

Imagine the ad campaign; it has changed little over thousands of years.

- We have all the answers.
- We have determined the path that must be followed in order to obtain salvation.
- We are the *only* ones that have it right; everyone else is wrong.

The key element of control is the constant reminder that one can neither do this on their own, nor by any other means, and the incessant reminder that evil is always just a thought away. It seems to matter little whether the leadership's postulates have any validity or value, or even truth, as long as there is a consensus that they do. I have pointed out elsewhere that the power of belief lies not in its truth, but in the universality of its acceptance.

The rhetoric of most religions teaches their members *about* God, or more simply stated someone's *opinions* about God. So, we have now reached the basis of Jung's statement. The persistent pursuit of reconciliation of the human dilemma by adopting the dogma of another, or a group of others, is a nonstarter, and is the perfect distraction from the fundamental realization that one is seeking.

That fundamental realization is described wonderfully by Krishnamurti in his writings:

> "Separation between God or reality and yourself is brought about by you, by the mind that clings to the known, to certainty, to security. This separation cannot be bridged over; there is no ritual, no discipline, no sacrifice that can carry you across it; there is no savior, no Master, no guru who can lead you to the real or destroy this separation. The division is not between the real and yourself, it is in yourself."

So almost as a postscript I will offer this opinion about the aforementioned dogma of Alcoholics Anonymous; if you are persistent in your pursuit of sobriety based on your understanding of how Bill Wilson did it, or how the leader of your group insists he does it, or how any of the other "AA celebrities" have done it, you will continue to miss the opportunity to turn around in your own shoes and investigate the "reality" of your own sobriety.

UNWORTHY (STEP 1)

This was originally written as pure satire. As I reread it now however and put myself in the shoes of a new member it is most poignant. How terrifying it would be to find oneself in that position of embattlement, and then self-perpetuate it by continuing to believe the non-sensical rantings of presumably "more sober" members of the group.

I AM SO GLAD THAT the new year has arrived. I have lots and lots of resolutions. I'm going to do the steps again! I've already begun to write out a first step; well, I haven't done any actual writing yet, but I've been thinking about it. A lot. I'm pretty sure it will be long because I want to make certain that I document every single example of the unmanageability of my life.

The one thing I really *have* been doing is concentrating on just how powerless I really am. You folks have been telling me for a long while that my best thinking got me here, that my mind is out to kill me, that my disease wants me dead, and that I had better keep that in mind. Always. It seems to be working too. I can see how focusing on that makes cunning, baffling, and powerful inadequate to describe it. Ferocious, relentless, and ruthless should be added to that. Oh, and patient. Nearly forgot that one. Oh, and insidious. Wow! This *is* some nasty business.

And how could I not have included the nefarious ego with all its shenanigans in the aforementioned list of things to be frightened of? I mean concerned with? I have been warned that without constant vigilance my ego will take my soul without my consent!

Now I'm beginning to think there may not be enough time in the day to do all that writing. All this vigilance, anxiety, and fear has pretty much consumed all my waking hours. But I think I'm finally getting this first step!

FAITH AND BELIEF

MOST OFTEN WHEN I HEAR discussions about the second step, folks have gone way beyond the sentiment of the step and are busy attempting to define God, or at the very least trying to reach some conclusions about what constitutes a belief. One of the most restricting of those old ideas that Bill suggests that some of us have tried to hold onto, is the notion that faith and belief are inextricably linked, i.e. that you cannot have faith without a belief to have faith in.

In the *Twelve and Twelve* Bill expounds on the step further, and there *his* comments are more relevant to faith than they are to belief. He, too, seems to use the two interchangeably. So what is faith?

Through the means of inductive reasoning, which establishes a *reasonable expectation* that certain things will continue to be simply because they have always been, we develop faith in all sorts of things and processes. Almost all of that is done with neither consciousness nor effort on our part. There is no need to believe that the sun will continue to make an appearance every day, we have faith that will be the case. The very ebb and flow of the universe goes virtually unnoticed. We seldom pause to think about, much less worry ourselves with, the faith we have that the universe will continue to unfold, and that this tiny speck of it that we have come to call the world, will continue to go round and round.

Faith, then, is inherently instinctive, and operates intuitively without our consciousness of it, or even the awareness of its existence. What then is the relationship between faith and belief? Lack of faith, or more accurately described, failing to recognize that intuitive faith, is the fertile soil in which the seeds of fear can sprout and quickly begin to grow.

When you get the egoic construct and the thinkingness of the mind involved, things can change rapidly. Lack of faith precipitates fear, and the mind creates hope to alleviate that fear. Hope is fueled by imagination, and as the hope grows so does the illusion. Because the illusion is so appealing and the hope so fervent, we begin to actually believe whatever it is that we have dreamed up.

As the dynamics of our lives change, new fears continually manifest themselves, and since by now we have very little faith in the way things are, we become more and more reliant on the hope that they will be different in the future.

Belief is nothing more than fervent hope. Oddly enough the traditional concepts of God have come from the *lack* of faith, not through it.

It does not require much faith to create or modify your concepts of God. A little imagination and some ego-driven desires are all that are needed. On the other hand, it is in the willingness to discard those antiquated perceptions that faith is essential.

YOGI'S STEP

WITHOUT SAYING SO SPECIFICALLY, THE second step, *"Came to believe that a power* greater *than ourselves could restore us to sanity,",* brings us to a fork in the road. Conventional AA wisdom suggests that you tell your naughty little self to shut up, sit down in the back seat, and then proceed on the path of righteousness.

I think Yogi Berra had a better idea: he suggested that when you come to a fork in the road, take it. The awareness of, and the willingness to investigate and pay attention to, the nature of this power that is other than ourselves, is the very essence of the path, or this spiritual journey if you wish to call it that. However, I think it would be an egregious error not to pay attention to and investigate the nature of this thing that we have always considered to be, "ourselves" as well.

To a mind that is conditioned to think in terms of duality—this or that, right or wrong, and so on—it seems impossible to travel both paths simultaneously. Nor does it seem at all likely that they may lead to the same place. So let us bow to logic and consider first one and then the other. And rather than flip a coin, let's defer to conventional wisdom and take the high road first.

Let's set aside altogether this business of belief for now and take a closer look at the faith and/or trust that have always been assumed to be an inherent part of belief. More to the point, let's consider:

1. The possibility that faith and belief are *not* inextricably linked and
2. That faith may well serve our purposes in a much more immediate and tangible way.

If you have been able to not drink for a few hours and maybe even a couple of days, and if during that time you have managed to sit through the initial anguish of a couple of meetings, take a look at that. A good look. There is a connection.

It's probable that you didn't even recognize the essence of Alcoholics Anonymous—the compassion that quietly and very subtly flows between drunks. Drunks that understand their own stories, and yours, as only drunks can. That sense of community and the feeling of being home at last is built on trust. Not only trust in each other, but trust in the process of AA.

So, the process itself begins to define that power that is other than ourselves, and the willingness to trust that process is the basis of the commitment to get involved in it. One day at a time we begin to take suggestions, and one day at a time we continue to not drink, and for most of us it comes as quite a surprise when a few of those days have been strung together. And here's an even bigger surprise: as we have become willing to trust others, and then trust the process, we have begun to develop some trust in ourselves.

So now we are back to ourselves, the perception and understanding of which is even more of a mystery than the "otherness" that we have just begun to explore. Bill himself opened the door of inquiry into this when he identified the "innermost self" as being the recipient of the concession that we are alcoholic.

There is good reason that Bill identifies that concession as the first step in recovery. I'm not sure that Bill thought about it at the time, and it is most unlikely that you will identify it at first, but that simple recognition that you are not the "body/mind" that you have always imagined yourself to be is the genesis of the most fundamental question in life: "who or what am I?"

So here we are back at the beginning, at the fork. The acknowledgement of this power other than ourselves, that is the common effort and the process itself, allows us to move forward in cleaning up the circumstances of our lives. And if we simultaneously inquire into the true nature of self, we begin to see just how much of the world that we were convinced was so overwhelming and hostile, was nothing more than our imagination and perception of it.

So, when you come to the fork in the road, take it! Turns out that the search for Truth, Reality, God, and the search for Self, are all the same. Enjoy the journey!

BACK TO BASICS

IF YOU HAVE BEEN AROUND Alcoholics Anonymous for any length of time, you have undoubtedly heard the term "back to basics." I suspect that most would agree that what that describes is staying in touch with the core values and the program of action that have been the backbone of AA from the beginning.

There *are* those however who have jumped onto the bandwagon of the most widely publicized and romanticized AA evangelist, Wally P., who insists that AA should return to, and remain grounded in, the teachings of the Oxford Group of the 1930's, and the reputed practices of 1940's Akron AA.

Even though I find those ideas preposterous, refuting them is not the purpose of this piece. The question I am dying to ask however, is why stop there? If we have access to some sort of magical time machine, why settle for a minuscule hop of less than a century? Let's truly get back to basics and visit the initial emergence of our cognitive ability!

Perhaps I should pause here and offer a disclaimer. I am not an expert on any of the opinions that follow. I have not been educated in evolutionary theory, evolutionary psychology, or any other psychology for that matter. I have read many differing opinions, offered by a wide range of others, concerning the very nature of many various and sundry things; but from that I have gleaned nothing more than some opinions of my own. The one thing that I am certain of however, is that I am curious. And that has led me forward to this.

There are a wide range of views among the various disciplines of the scientific and historical communities regarding the time frame as to when we as a species first began to notice that we were developing the capacity to "figure things out." When it occurred is not terribly important; that it *did* occur is monumental.

I believe the ever-increasing ability to figure things out and the insatiable desire to continue to do so has been the driving force behind the evolution of our species ever since.

Initially that ability would most certainly have been a boon to the success of the hunting and/or gathering of the day. The memory of past circumstances culminating in specific results would have increased the ability to predict similar future results. Even though the fostering of that simple ability has led to the astounding evolution of our brains themselves, and to the almost incomprehensible accomplishments that we have achieved as the result, that is not what I would like to focus on here.

Unfortunately, there is a flip side to that insatiable desire to figure things out—the fear that you may not be able to. The seemingly endless cycle of fear and desire quickly began to manifest itself out of that dichotomy. It can simply be defined as the desire to figure things out, and the nagging suspicion that you are failing miserably in your efforts to do so.

I cannot imagine a more fundamental sense of the human dilemma than the shock of finding oneself alive without having the slightest clue about how to navigate through the experience of it.

Now. We are back to basics.

So, what's a human to do?

Initially, it must have been quite comforting to find oneself among others, or even just one other, who seemed to be more proficient with this cognitive ability. Consider if you will, the value that must have quickly been assigned to that capacity. That ability became currency, and would most certainly have furthered the delineation between the haves and have-nots.

The almost unwitting concession by most of the members of the early bands of humans; that someone else was better equipped or more qualified to handle affairs that they themselves felt inadequate to deal with, had to have been the genesis of the evolution of culture itself.

The initial enculturation of like-minded people into groups would have been aided greatly by the increasing specialization that would have begun to exhibit itself in those early bands. One person may have been unusually athletic, and thus a superior hunter; another may have been more adept at fashioning clothing or rudimentary footwear. There were likely some who were better suited to childcare than either gathering or cooking, and vice versa.

It is likely that bartering quickly became common-place. There were also no doubt some who had no interest in any of the more mundane aspects of survival but had begun to cash in on the currency of "I can figure things out." The village know-it-all—shaman and/or politician—began to emerge.

Ideas themselves became a marketable commodity; people were willing to trade other goods and services for the reassurance that someone else was figuring things out, releasing them of the responsibility. What a relief!

The original brokers in thinking must surely have begun to feel the pressure of that acquiescence, however. In order to maintain their credibility, it would have been incumbent upon them to continue to come up with the goods. Since they undoubtedly began to run out of things that they *could* figure out, they simply would have begun to make things up.

It's not necessary for me to go into any great detail about ideas and beliefs that would have been readily accepted at one time, that are considered to be absurd today. The fact is that much of that original ideology would have initially been accepted simply because of its venerated source.

The fundamental and most basic dilemma of being human has not changed for tens of thousands of years, nor have the most common of the attempts to resolve the issue: either deferring to someone else's presumed abilities or avoiding the matter altogether.

So. Since it appears that the usefulness of this field trip into the past seems to be waning, let's get back to the present!

One of the most evident differences between our current circumstances and those of generations gone by, is that not only have we figured a lot of things out, we also have easy access to almost any and all of that accrued knowledge.

The dilemma has evolved also. It's no longer focused primarily upon solving the riddles of surviving the physical challenges of life, we have the benefit of having accomplished a great deal in that regard.

The quandary is now more subtle: that sense of dis-ease seems to have settled mostly below the level of consciousness. Most of us are not even sure what the questions should be, let alone how to find any answers. However, that subtle sense of discomfort continues to find its way into our awareness, often at the most inopportune moments.

One thing seems clear: Figuring it out doesn't appear to be the solution to not being able to figure it out. In fact, attempting to *think* one's way out of this conundrum could be likened to the effort to extract one's fingers from the woven bamboo tube affec-tionately known as Chinese handcuffs. The more you struggle, the more tightly bound you become.

Another result of humans' many accomplishments is the unprecedented amount of free time that mod-ern technologies afford us. On the surface that would seem to be most welcome. The other side of that coin however, presents us with two of the questions that are inherent to the dilemma: what now, and what's next?

Most of us seem to be more than a little uncomfortable with all that free time, and consequently spend a lot of it looking for more creative ways to fill it. Another way to describe that vague sense of discomfort is to recognize that from a neurological point of view, the sense of becoming is much more rewarding than the sense of being. Simply being still (or satisfied) literally goes against basic human nature.

As you will recall, I opened this piece with reference to "back to basics" as it pertains to Alcoholics Anonymous. So, it only seems fitting that I now pose a question that is asked regularly by a friend of mine:

> "What the hell does any of that have to do with me drinking warm vodka from a plastic bottle that has been ever-so-cleverly concealed in a brown paper bag?"

Everything. Absolutely everything.

For millions of people, it has been that drink, at least initially, that so effectively washes away the most fundamental sense of dis-ease that I have been attempting to describe.

Without getting too deeply involved in any of the opinions about what alcoholism is or isn't, or what treatment may or may not be effective or even helpful, I think there would likely be a general consensus among those that are familiar with the malady that in the case of an alcoholic, what initially seems to be the solution, ultimately becomes the problem.

That seems to be true with many of the other methods that we have learned to employ. I use the word "distraction" for any and all of those means—ranging from the seemingly harmless urge to fiddle with your smartphone to the debilitating nightmare of full-blown addiction.

Alcoholism seems to be the gold standard here. On occasion even the nomenclature has been borrowed; for example, shopaholic, workaholic, and sexaholic etc.

It is especially important here to notice that by the time the presupposed solution has become the problem, the focus has shifted to the *new* problem, and the original dilemma has been all but forgotten. The new problem and the search for its solution, become an even more effective distraction from the original predicament. (Tug a little harder on those handcuffs!)

Back to basics should imply recognizing the futility of being focused exclusively on the problems presented by any or all of the distractions that we have been engaged in, and the willingness to begin to examine the dilemma itself.

Shifting to this new perspective can be difficult. The nature of the dilemma thwarts its resolution and ensures its perpetuity. The instinctive urge to *fix* the problem must be set aside in order to begin to *understand* it.

At this point it would be very tempting to trot out opinions and quotes from any number of sages, teachers, and mystics, from both past and present, whose words would lend credence to what I am about to suggest. However, there is only one word that describes this proposal.

And the proposal is very simple: Stop.

If this were an audio presentation, there would be a pause here. A long one. The only way that I can think to accomplish that on a written page, however, would be to leave it blank, and I smile as I think of folks simply skipping over it to get to "what's next."

What's next is the willingness to look at the resistance we all seem to feel at the very thought of being still.

Again, the temptation is to point to the wisdom of some of the Eastern teachings, or to cite more current opinions from the disciplines of psychology and neuroscience, that would indicate that the most common ideas that we have always entertained about the notion of self are false. But there is really no need to make this all that complicated.

In the simplest of terms, I think it would be safe to say that most of us tend to identify the sense of self in no small part with the thinking-ness of our minds. At the most fundamental level, we have become dependent upon a mind that has been conditioned by the cultures that we have found ourselves in.

I am certainly not qualified to speak about any other culture, but this one, the one I find myself in here and now, is very goal oriented. We have been offered anything and everything desirable in life (and for some even beyond this life) on the contingency plan. We are being promised continually that happiness, freedom, security, and that coveted sense of well-being will be ours—if and when. . .

That mindset not only comes from, but it is also continuously fueled by, the basic dilemma that I have been describing. The underlying fear comes from non-acceptance of what *is*. But the *effort* to accept what is puts us back on the treadmill, with the hope that the future will somehow be different.

One of my favorite interpretations of the *Tao Te Ching* is Stephen Mitchel's *New English Version*. Here I am paraphrasing an excerpt from chapter 13 of that interpretation: "Hope is as hollow as fear, simply because both arise from the illusion of self."

Hope is another (and probably the most often used) way of avoiding the fear that seems to underlie the very sense of self. However, just as another payday loan is never the permanent solution for a budgeting crisis, another bushel of hope does not provide enduring relief from the fears that have driven our lives. As new fears arise, and the old ones continue to nag, the hopes we had covered them with begin to wear thin, and once again we anxiously embark on the search for another fix, and yet another. . .

It is inevitable that the unresolved fears continue to accumulate, and more hope is required to maintain any sense of balance. The consequence of that is finding ourselves spending much more of our time in the fantasies of the future, than in the reality of the present. In fact, it would seem that most of us are making a valiant attempt to stay one step ahead of our lives, out of fear that what we have imagined them to be comes up painfully short when compared to what we have always been told they should be.

The illusion is that without the concerted effort to become something more, the fear of being less than our heart's desire will somehow become reality.

The suggestion to stop is offered as the gentlest of invitations. Being still, even briefly, affords the opportunity to literally step out of the picture, and realize the futility of the never-ending chase. The realization is that even though the urge to participate in the constant pursuit of something more is as natural as breathing, it is not nearly as necessary.

At the most basic level, the dilemma can be seen as a fundamental part of the mystery of being human—a mystery that has yet to be solved, even though there are always innumerable folks working feverishly toward that end. I pay very little attention to what passes for news these days, but I am fairly certain that if any of those sleuths are ever successful, I will hear about it.

In the meantime, I am content with not knowing. I don't have any expectations of finding definitive answers to deep philosophical questions such as "who am I?", or "what is the true nature of self?", but I have been able to discard a lot of other people's opinions on those matters, as I have recognized them to be nothing *more* than opinions.

The ability to live life as it unfolds without undue concern about what was or should have been, or what hopefully will be or should be, is the result. It is a sense of just being. Which points to this most enigmatic statement that I can imagine; the sense of being cannot be attained through any effort. It is realized by letting go of both the fear of *not being* and the desire to *become*.

That is the resolution of the human dilemma.

TWELVE

12... BEING MORE THAN A little disappointed with not having had much of a noticeable spiritual awakening as the result of these steps, we immediately went back to the beginning and started over; hoping to relieve some of the nervousness we felt about the possibility of not having done them correctly, or the genuine concern about not having been thorough enough. There was a nagging suspicion that there may have been details that we could have missed; but most of all we were terrified of being caught without the proper amount of maintenance or having been tempted to spend a couple of days laurel resting. After all, the message is repeated in nearly every meeting, and the accompanying insinuation is very clear; if you *ever* get off the treadmill, your disease will surely club you upside the head and drag you into the nearest barroom.

I suspect that even those who subscribe to that mindset will find it a bit disconcerting to hear it described that way. The subtleties of that outlook come from the religious model of AA—a model borrowed without apology from the Abrahamic religions. Regardless of whether you choose to acknowledge it, traditional AA promises rewards for compliance and punishment for any disobedience. Even if you don't drink, you could easily find yourself in the netherworld of *dry* drunkenness.

When looked at from a historical viewpoint, that attitude is easily explained. Alcoholics Anonymous was born within a culture that embraced those very ideals. God and religion were seen as the remedy for all the ills of society, and the drunken misbehavior of the alcoholics was certainly no exception. So almost by default, the doctrine of AA is modeled after those ideals. There were non-believers to be sure, but I suspect that at least some of the folks that *didn't* believe, either knew they should, or wished that they could; and those that *did* believe seemed certain that with enough prodding and a little patience, they would be able to help the wayward ones see the error of their ways. Bill wrote about that very thing in his essay on step two in *Twelve Steps and Twelve Traditions* and wrote a whole chapter in the book *Alcoholics Anonymous* for those folks. He claimed that it was to the agnostics, and entitled the chapter accordingly, but it really appears to have been written to the convertibles.

The other historical point of perspective is perhaps even more relevant. When the book *Alcoholics Anonymous* was published in April of 1939, there were precious few who had more than just a few months of sobriety; all told it seems there were likely fewer than a hundred. As breathtaking and exciting as their newfound sobriety was, there was little precedent to suggest that it could be sustained. Their nervousness about early sobriety was certainly justified, and the jump to the conclusion that they had better continue to follow the recipe verbatim was not illogical at all.

I certainly wouldn't suggest that there was no one who had begun to realize the state of simply being sober and being comfortable with it, but that attitude did not make its way into the book. The book, which today unfortunately, is seen by many to be holy scripture.

So why this resistance to the evolution of sobriety as it unfolds, and the insistence that AA remain tethered to the milieu from whence it came?

I suspect the answer to that question may be much simpler than we ever could have imagined. We simply seem to be genetically inclined to struggle!

It's not difficult to identify the conflicts and the accompanying struggles of our ancient ancestors, whether it was with nature, or with each other, as being matters of life and death. Quite often the stakes were incredibly high; it was not win or lose, it was win or die.

Much of the basic mistrust and the wariness of life has been carried forward not only culturally, but perhaps even in our DNA. Our modern cultures seem to have eliminated, or at least mollified, most of those physical dangers that were apt to have kept our ancestors in turmoil, but they have added immeasurably to the list of things for us to be concerned with.

Psychologist and Buddhist meditation teacher Tara Brach offers some wonderful insight into the additional struggles that our Western cultures have given us.

> "Our culture's guiding myth is the story of Adam and Eve's exile from the Garden of Eden. We may forget its power because it seems so worn and familiar, but this story shapes and reflects the deep psyche of the West. The message of "original sin" is unequivocal: Because of our basically flawed nature, we do not deserve to be happy, loved by others, at ease with life. We are outcasts, and if we are to reenter the garden, we must redeem our sinful selves. We must overcome our flaws by controlling our bodies, controlling our emotions, controlling our natural surroundings, controlling other people. And we must strive tirelessly—working, acquiring, consuming, achieving, e-mailing, over committing, and rushing—in a never-ending quest to prove ourselves once and for all." *(Radical Acceptance p. 12)*

In short, it's not OK to be OK.

You don't have to look too deeply into the doctrine of AA to see how closely it parallels the underlying anguish that is so vividly described by Ms. Brach. Our cultural conditioning has given us a sense of nervousness about the existence of a never-ending struggle between the forces of good and evil; at times almost indiscernible, yet seemingly always there.

It's important to recognize that that nervousness is a cultural phenomenon, not limited to those who are involved in the practice of religion. This nagging suspicion also influences our perception of social and political arenas. Consider how much easier it is to justify your fear of, and/or dislike for, someone if you can place him or her, or *them,* on the "evil" side of the ledger. A superb way to rationalize an "Us and Them" attitude.

Bill perpetuates that uneasiness with his descriptions of alcoholism. He quite literally creates the bogeyman that is "alcohol-ISM" with the ominous and foreboding images he paints with his colorful language, and modern AA, (with a little help from the treatment industry), has refined that notion into "my disease," which can be, and with astonishing regularity is, blamed for an incredible assortment of unseemly thoughts and actions.

The result of that bogeyman mentality is the conviction that you can never just be. Being overrun by the Dark Side is seen as inevitable unless you are constantly moving; Progress not perfection, daily reprieve, every day is the day you must... etc.

My intent here is not to diminish the importance of getting involved with the process of recovery as laid out in the steps. Nor is it to insinuate that one can view them (the steps) simply as items to be checked from a "to do" list and then forgotten. And I am certainly not suggesting that there is a shortcut from drunken nightmare on Tuesday to meditative bliss on Friday.

What I *am* suggesting however, is that comfortable and sustainable sobriety is possible without remaining stuck in the original regimen. There is no need to hone the on-going process into the maintenance of a ridged, inculcated ritual that must be repeated interminably in order to enjoy the experience of *being* sober.

Although it differs considerably from the spiritual condition that Bill so painfully describes, and insists must be maintained, this description from Adyashanti more clearly describes my experience.

> "Spirituality does not require that you work hard toward achieving a result in the future as much as it requires you to be fully present, sincere, and committed now, with absolute honesty and a willingness to uncover and let go of any illusion that comes between you and the realization of Reality. Therefore, spirituality does not have to do with time or what can be achieved in time; it has to do only and always with the eternal present."

Therein lies a very short and sweet synopsis of the steps: "uncover and let go of any illusion." ..

The steps are nothing more than a means of self-examination. If engaged thoroughly, they can reveal insights into the very nature of the ways we have viewed, and then responded to, the circumstances of our lives. Most importantly, we can see how those responses can be altered simply by shifting the way we perceive things. And that shift in perspective is no more complicated than changing our minds, or as Bill suggested, letting go of old ideas.

However, even with that acknowledgement, it seems to me that the steps are most often viewed with a cause-and-effect mentality. The problem with that mindset is with the expectations that we create by looking at them in that way. The notion may be subtle or even subconscious, but the idea that there will be a prize or a reward is hard to ignore. Regardless of how you define a spiritual awakening, Bill set the bar extremely high with that being the promise.

One of the more unfortunate myths that have evolved since the early days of AA is the insistence that the steps are numbered for a reason and should therefore be approached in order, and in a very linear fashion. I have yet to hear a compelling argument for that.

I see no reason to wait until you are three-quarters of the way through the steps before you begin to pay attention (step 10) and seek to cultivate some stillness (step 11). The essence of those two steps combined is what an ever-increasing number of current seekers refer to as mindfulness. (The Buddha spoke extensively about that in his teachings, but that's a story for another time.)

When utilized from the beginning, that mindfulness can completely change the perspective of the process. Instead of being a series of arduous tasks that must be completed, (influenced significantly by the nervousness about passing each and every exam along the way), the steps can be seen as the path to truths to be discovered. Truths about ourselves; truths that we begin to realize have always been known but have been steeply discounted or simply ignored all together.

Minimizing the expectation of what will be, or should be, can give us a greater opportunity to be aware of, and in tune with, what is. Rather than viewing the process as "doing" the steps, or "working" the steps, we can gradually begin to realize a sense of simply building a relationship with them, and ultimately that relationship becomes the experience of being sober.

The essence and the wisdom of these steps are not to be found in the words that describe them. The proof, as they say, is "in the pudding." It is highly unlikely that the taste of an apple pie can be experienced by chewing on the recipe.

The result of this process turns out to be no result at all. The steps, individually and collectively, are simply additional points of awareness on the continuum of our lives. The folks who define their sobriety as "living in ten, eleven, and twelve" are describing nothing more than the mindfulness that I mentioned earlier.

There are a host of catch phrases that are glibly tossed about in an effort to describe living a comfortable life without alcohol; there is no need to repeat any of them here. My experience is all that need be described, and it is nothing more than this:

TWELVE

From the stillness that I spoke of earlier, comes the recognition of a deep sense of being, and that sense emanates very simply from the profound realization that I am.

THE CONDITION MY CONDITION IS IN

IN THE SECOND OF THE four paragraphs in which Bill describes step 10 *(Alcoholics Anonymous pages 84 and 85),* he introduces a wonderful position of neutrality. He describes having dropped most, if not all, resistance to *what is*. He describes no longer having any quarrel with anyone or anything, and suggests that we have ceased fighting everything, even alcohol! But then in the very next paragraph he reminds us that alcohol is a subtle foe. I can't help but point out that it is not really surrender if you are still willing to fight, regardless of how subtle the foe may or may not be.

Also in that third paragraph is what may be the lynchpin for the religious model of AA. "What we really have is a daily reprieve contingent on the maintenance of our spiritual condition."

You may be surprised to learn that the definition of reprieve (in every dictionary I consulted) is a stay of execution. I picture not a pardon with a handshake and an apology along with an invitation to "have a nice life," but instead being shuffled back to a cell with yet another reminder that the governor still hasn't made up his mind. And along with that, the conciliatory suggestion to be sure to "call again tomorrow."

I will consider that to be a side note however, and not even pause to consider the various interpretations of either contingent or maintenance, so as to more quickly get to the heart of the matter which must surely be this spiritual condition.

The perception of what constitutes a spiritual condition for me vs. what constituted the same for Bill Wilson, would be grounds for endless discussion. However, since having that discussion with Bill is off the table, I will refer here to his written word. I can only assume that all of the exhortations contained in the other three of the four paragraphs on step 10, and the litany of explicit instructions that are listed on the next two and a half pages with regard to step 11, were Bill's ideas about what would have been required to sustain a proper program of maintenance.

Since virtually all of those requirements are so firmly entrenched in the theological traditions of the West, I assume that Bill's ideas about this "spiritual condition" rested upon the same foundation.

There's the rub. What if my spiritual condition is not based on the dogma of the Abrahamic religions? What if it is based simply on my sense of being, not on the frantic and never-ending attempts to become?

That certainly seems to be a conundrum. How can one possibly get to be without the effort to become? Oddly enough, Bill offers some direction for that.

In what I have come to refer to as the closing argument (*Alcoholics Anonymous p.164*), he offers what is perhaps the simplest yet most profound of all the instructions in the book: "Abandon yourself to God."

Notice that I have placed the period *there,* even though Bill goes on to suggest that it can be "God as you understand God." That addendum in and of itself is the source of all sorts of confusion as it insinuates that there is an understanding possible and getting caught up in the pursuit of that understanding can lead to innumerable detours. While your learning *about* God can provide some sense of relief, it hardly ever provides the complete satisfaction that is being sought. And even when it seems to, it is fleeting at best. But enough about that, let's get back to the original premise.

First of all, please note that there are three aspects of this proposition. Since action seems to be held in such high regard in and around AA, let's begin with a look at the verb. The first definition of abandon in the *Oxford American Dictionary* is "to give up completely." Sounds a bit like surrender to me; in fact, the same dictionary opines that to surrender is to "abandon oneself entirely."

The fundamental problem with this idea of abandonment, as any hoarder worth his salt will tell you, is that it is impossible to abandon *anything* if there is even a remote possibility of it having any intrinsic value— either now or in the future. To further complicate matters, it seems to matter very little whether that value is real or imagined.

So let's consider the softer language of step three which suggests "turning it over"; somehow that doesn't seem so difficult, and maybe not so final. But that idea comes with its own complications and consequences. Simply turning it over allows me to hold onto the possibility of monitoring the results of having turned it over, and I can also reserve the right to compare the results of my having turned it over with my expectations of turning it over, thereby giving myself the option of judging the effectiveness of this entire "turning it over" business. Whew! Doesn't sound like much of a surrender at all does it?

So, let's make this concession; this surrender/abandonment concept seems to be fairly pedestrian in theory, but actually doing it requires some effort. I would like to suggest that earnestness and diligence are appropriate descriptions of that ongoing effort.

Acknowledging that this abandonment process is not going to be a one-and-done, or a flip-a-switch, sort of thing will allow us to set it aside for now and move on, so let's take a look at the other two aspects of the suggestion.

I suppose that most would agree that God would seem to be the more important of the remaining two, so let's go there next. Maybe the prospect of abandonment would be a bit more palatable if we *did* have some understanding of this God business. Virtually all of us have some concept of God, if only because of the cultural conditioning we have all been given so freely.

I would suggest that some of the most debilitating of the "old ideas" that Bill suggests that many of us have tried to hold on to are those concepts. The key here is to truly investigate those old ideas, not just trade them in for newer models.

Please consider here what I pointed out earlier as far as knowing *about* God. Proposition C (the last of the three pertinent ideas), is about seeking God; not seeking knowledge of God. It's not about comparing notes from various religions and/or cultures, nor is it about the validity of any of the fairy tales that you have been told about who or what God is; nor is it about any sort of magic that any deity may or may not be capable of. This seeking business is not an intellectual pursuit. That quest can only perpetuate your entanglement with someone *else's* sentiments and ideas about God.

So if, and granted this is a big if, you can concede that any traditional concept of God is simply someone else's *opinion* of what God is, and that no human mind is capable of truly comprehending the essence of what God must be, then you can gradually relax into the reality that God simply is—with or without that particular name.

So, what's left? The adventure of a lifetime.

Bill states on page 30, *(Alcoholics Anonymous),* that conceding to our innermost selves that we are alcoholic is the first step in recovery. I would suggest that conceding to our innermost selves that we have no idea what this innermost self *is*, is the first step out of the *illusion* of self.

Traditional AA makes this whole process one of self-improvement. You must first recognize that you have been a naughty little self, then say you're sorry and make an endless and concerted effort to fix yourself. Remember the original suggestion is about the abandonment of self, not the judgment of it; it's not about reprimanding it, nor correcting it, and most certainly not about punishing it.

The problem inherent with the traditional self-improvement idea is this: The more time and effort you exert in the attempt to fix the self, the more consumed you become with your own damned *Self!!*

Rather than relying on the assumption that we know what this "self" is and continue the never-ending drudgery of trying to discipline it, we may find it much more profitable to admit that we know very little about this mysterious essence we have always referred to as self.

I am certainly not qualified to expound on the opinions of modern psychology, nor those of neuroscience; nor am I an expert on the opinions offered by any of the wide and varied theological and philosophical traditions.

What I am qualified to speak about however is my own experience, and one of the most important events in that collective experience was the moment of truth when I realized that everything I had ever been told or had read was simply someone's opinion.

Everything.

In that moment, an incredible journey began. It can be described simply as having found the willingness to question everything. One of the most astounding areas of that investigation is the question of self. Who or what am I? I really don't know. As the result of that realization however, all of the previous conditioning began to unravel. All that I had ever been told, not only about who I am, but even more importantly about who I am *supposed* to be, was brought into question.

One of the real astonishing things that began to become evident is that I had never been given a complete overview of any of it. I had simply picked up clues, many of which may or may not have been intended to be understood in the way in which I had interpreted them, and then with my imagination I filled in the blanks.

I quite literally imagined myself to be the product of my own imagination! That is the illusion of self that I mentioned earlier.

I did not begin this piece with the intent of it being instructive in any particular way. There simply cannot be a journey more personal than the journey into the nature of one's own self. Nor did I intend to make this a treatise on steps ten and eleven, but that's where I find myself now.

I have written elsewhere about my views on the simplicity of those two steps. Step ten is nothing more than paying attention, and eleven is simply about cultivating some stillness; (my opinion of course.) The result of melding the two is what many modern seekers refer to as mindfulness. As valuable as each is on its own, both concepts are exponentially more powerful when fused together.

As I became more adept at quieting the mind, it became easier to focus on individual thoughts, and question their origin and their validity. Through that awareness I began to see that my troubles are indeed of my own making. And that the vast majority of those troubles have come from believing my own thoughts.

So, this abandonment of self is really about the abandonment of the *ideas* about self. When those old ideas are recognized as being false, and seen to have no value, letting them go requires very little effort. One of the most amazing and totally unexpected consequences of this process is that since they, too, are based on the illusion, many of the fears and desires of the false self simply fade away as well.

To my way of thinking, the aforementioned position of neutrality *is* the result of these steps and is in fact the spiritual condition that is worthy of maintenance. Interestingly enough, the maintenance of a position of neutrality is ridiculously simple. There are no upper levels of neutrality—no "super neutral" to strive for. In the simplest of terms, maintaining neutrality is accomplished by simply remaining neutral.

The effort is toward deepening the awareness and the stillness, and thereby recognizing when the circumstances of life tend to draw us out of it. Even the most mundane and unpleasant events of our lives can be attended to mindfully. A large part of the critical awareness is recognizing that the details of our lives do need attention, and that it is much less distracting to pay attention immediately, rather than putting presumed unpleasantries off until that attention is demanded. Those demands can easily become quite uncomfortable and needlessly complicated and are often accompanied by chaos and conflict; and when the chaos and conflict become too overwhelming, it is all too easy to engage in fantasies about how it should have been, the unfairness of life, whose fault it is or was, and so on and on it goes. Those fantasies simply serve as further distractions from the reality of what is.

But here is the really good news: this mindful view of life is not something that can and will occur sometime in the future after you have completed all of the requirements and proven yourself worthy. It is happening. Now. It's not about what was, nor is it about what might be—it is always about what is.

As I have pondered how best to draw all this together and bring it to some conclusion, the most meaningful thing that comes to mind is to extend the heartfelt invitation that I accepted all those years ago.

Learn to be still.

LEARNING

FOR MANY YEARS I HAVE described my path as having been nothing more complicated than learning to be still; and for most of those years I have used the quaint phrase "hunky-damned-dory" to describe the essence of that stillness. Quite often I have noted that that "hunky-damned-dory"-ness has become the default position. By default, I mean that state of consciousness where nothing is pending; where there is no imminent need for either thought or action.

As you may well imagine, it has been difficult to describe that stillness, particularly to folks who have never even considered the possible usefulness of such a thing. In no small part because of that difficulty, it has often been frustrating to participate in the innumerable discussions that I have been party to, (both private and at a group level), about the concept of learning to be still.

It has occurred to me recently however that virtually all those discussions have been centered around, and were focused upon, the stillness. As I pondered that a bit, I realized that it is not only about the stillness, the learning itself is equally important.

There is a brusque command in the gilded pages of that fancy book with the leather binding to "Be still and know that I am God." My response to that is, "Mind your own damned business" (PG version).

However, even after dismissing that, there still seems to be an enigmatic appeal to the gentle suggestion to "learn to be still."

Most folks naturally equate learning with the acquisition of knowledge. That certainly holds true for the technical knowledge that has been the genesis, and is the result of, the evolution of our species, and is unquestionably necessary for us to function in our everyday lives.

That's not what I am referring to here. The learning that I am speaking of is the almost accidental realization of something. Let me offer a rudimentary example.

See if you can recall that moment when you suddenly realized that you were riding a bicycle for the first time. Regardless of how much effort had been expended prior to that, or how much teaching and coaching you had received, or even how many times you had tried and failed, the actual experience of riding was the learning. The experience of riding and the learning to ride were one and the same.

If you now ponder not the actual riding of the bike, but the initial experience of it, you may be able to see the essence of the learning itself. Most importantly you can see that there was no thinking involved in the event. The old ideas of self-doubt and fear had been set aside, along with the expectations of what the experience was going to be like. Without the intellect involved, the whole occurrence became experiential.

In much the same way, the notion of learning to be still offers a delightful conundrum wherein the stillness seems to be contingent upon the learning, yet the learning itself is the experience of the stillness. The more engaged the mind is with ideas about how to become still, the further away from the stillness you are; and the more you entertain yourself with expectations of what this stillness will be like, the more likely it is that you will continue to miss the point.

The fact is, the stillness that I am talking about is always there—always has been, always will be. So quite often the initial experience of it may be just a glimpse, and the sudden awareness of it may seem accidental. But if we are paying attention, that glimpse is sure to pique some curiosity. The key here is the paying of attention.

The point is this: only when you have no idea what you're looking for, will you be open enough to recognize that you have always been what you have been trying so desperately to become.

And that realization can come as quite a shock—to find yourself at peace, in your own heart and with your own mind. Literally, in tune with the entire universe.

Bayezid Basmati, a Sufi mystic and philosopher, described this dilemma with this observation in the middle of the ninth century:

> "These truths we speak of cannot be found by seeking; yet only those that seek will find them."

A SNIPPET

I'M SURE THAT MOST OF us have seen the TV commercials that ask this rhetorical question: "Wouldn't it be nice if people said what they really meant?"

If Bill had said what he really meant, the twelfth step would read something like this: "Having had a religious conversion as the result of these steps, we enthusiastically joined the ranks of missionaries and tried to convert every damned newcomer we could get our hands on."

Facetious of course, but the point is this: Alcoholics Anonymous was born within a culture and at a time when God and religion were seen as the remedy for all the ills of society, and the drunken misbehavior of the alcoholics was certainly no exception. So almost by default, the doctrine of AA is modeled after those ideals. There were non-believers to be sure, but I suspect that at least some of the folks that *didn't* believe, either knew they should, or wished that they could. Bill wrote about that very thing in step two in *Twelve Steps and Twelve Traditions,* and included an entire chapter in the book *Alcoholics Anonymous* for those folks. He claimed that it was to the agnostics, and entitled that chapter accordingly, but it really appears to have been written to the convertibles.

When looked at in that light, neither the tone nor the content of the chapter *We Agnostics* is as condescending as it seems to be. One thing *is* clear however, it was not written by an agnostic, nor was it Bill's intent to reassure those of agnostic persuasion that it was possible to reap the benefits of this whole process without being converted.

0.5

I HAVE WRITTEN ELSEWHERE ABOUT what I have fondly referred to as step 0.5, and what Bill references on page 30 *(Alcoholics Anonymous)* as the first step in recovery. I.e., "We learned that we had to fully concede to our innermost selves that we were alcoholics."

My opinion about that may well be worth repeating here.

If that concession is in fact "full", then the accompanying surrender is also. This goes much deeper than "admitting", and even beyond accepting. I think a sense of agreement most accurately describes that surrender. This agreement is very matter of fact, without any emotional or intellectual deliberation. There has been neither bargaining, nor negotiation; and it is not a compromise. There is no anger, no self-pity, nor is there resentment toward those that *can* drink. It is simply the awareness that what is *is*.

This surrender, or sense of agreement, is not an event, but is more a shift in consciousness. In a very real sense, it *is* that psychic change. To come into agreement with being an alcoholic and looking honestly at what that means, is to also come into agreement with taking the steps necessary to literally alter the course of your life.

When seen from this viewpoint, alcoholism is no longer the enemy, nor is it an excuse. It can simply be accepted as the disease that it is and recognized as the explanation for the insanity that our lives had become. So, this "Spiritual Awakening" is not some mysterious mystical future event to be placed up on a shelf with all the other things that will hopefully make your life comfortable someday. The *experience,* call it spiritual if you like, begins with that concession, and the willingness to come into agreement with life. All of life.

The importance of that concession is obvious. Maybe *not* so obvious however, is the difference in perspective that can be gained as the result of it. It may be short lived, and perhaps not even fully understood at the time, but the relief that comes with that concession is not the result of *doing* anything. There has been no victory, no conquest, no triumph over alcohol; the relief is simply the result of dropping all resistance to being an alcoholic.

When recognized and then embraced, that mindset can become the basis of a change in attitude toward the entire process and can ultimately become the foundation for a totally unexpected approach to life moving forward.

In addition to the relief that comes with that agreement, consider for a moment all the energy that is now available. Energy that had previously been spent arguing with the reality of what is. That energy, when redirected, is the very foundation of this other power—the power that is described very specifically on pages

569/570 (*Alcoholics Anonymous third edition*) as an "unsuspected inner resource."

STILL SMALL VOICE

Pure satire.

THIS PAST WEEKEND, AFTER MANY years of earnest and diligent seeking, I imagined that I had at last gotten through to God. The conversation went something like this:

Still small voice: "Did you need something?"

Me: "Oh wow what a surprise! I was just wondering what your will is for me!"

Still small voice: "Didn't I tell you?"

Me (with great anticipation): "NO!"

Still small voice: "Then I guess it's none of your business."

PERSONAL PARABLES

THE MASTERS OF MOST, IF not all, Wisdom Traditions have used parables as teaching tools. Until recently (in the big scheme of things), the spoken word was the primary means of keeping those traditions alive, thereby assuring their place in the future.

As life lessons go, most can be pretty boring. If cut and dried and then laid out in a straight forward way, it can be difficult for their teachers to hold the attention or interest of anyone. If, however, those mentors employ some literary and poetic license and create a fable, or a story, with a plot, some characters, a little drama, and perhaps a twist at the end, it is quite likely that not only can the life lesson then be embedded, often it will have some added value.

I offer that brief history lesson as a prelude to this, a story from my teen age years.

Several times during each of the two summers during my high school years, I joined a group of friends who would somehow manage to get a substantial amount of beer rounded up, and then head up the canyon to spend the weekend at the lake. The remainder of the ritual involved renting a ramshackle cabin, and an even more dilapidated old wooden rowboat. The daytime hours were then spent out on the lake with fishing lines in the water, while we drank beer, smoked cigars, and pretended to be grownups.

As one of those glorious days was drawing to a close, and we were making our way back to the dock, I very proudly announced that I could swim faster than we seemed able to row the rickety old boat. I don't recall exactly how it occurred, but I soon found myself proving that. It wasn't long before I discovered that it is possible to drink a lot of beer while sitting around telling fish stories, without realizing just how drunk you may be getting. As that reality dawned on me, so did the realization that I was now halfway between the boat and the shore, and that I was in serious trouble.

I redoubled my effort and began to swim even more furiously toward the shore. It was not long before I was exhausted and even more frightened. I was still a couple dozen yards from the shore, but I could go no further. Suddenly I remembered a lesson from the lifesaving course that I had taken as a Boy Scout a few years earlier. That lesson was about a technique known as bobbing. The gist of that is to curl up into a ball, take a deep breath and then just relax. If you happen to go under, there is no need worry about it; when you bob back up you simply take another breath. The instructors insisted that it was possible to survive for hours that way, and that it was actually quite restful.

My panic subsided, my resolve began to return, and I bobbed. I can't describe my amazement as I curled up, submerged, and hit the bottom! When I stood up, the water was just to the middle of my chest!

When the memory of that event appeared in my consciousness several years ago, I smiled, maybe even giggled a little, at the foolishness of youth. For some inexplicable reason however, I spent some time with it, and as I sat with those memories, and their implications, I recognized a much deeper significance.

What arose out of that contemplation is this: that was the first occasion that I recall having taken the time and having paid full attention to what I now refer to as my own personal parables, and what was embedded in *that* parable was this rhetorical question; how much of my life have I spent swimming franticly in water that is only waist deep?

YOU *HAVE* TO CARE!

SEVERAL YEARS BEFORE MY RETIREMENT, I was working as a foreman on a job I was not particularly fond of.

The company I was working for had come from the late nineteenth century, and so had (at least in my opinion) some of their ludicrous methods. Of these antiquated procedures, the one that most pertained to me and my work, was their system of tracking costs, which in turn led to cost estimates, and ultimately to future bids.

That seemed to have been badly broken for years, but it appeared that no one with enough authority to change anything was willing to admit it. Because of that, no one ever actually reported costs. It had become necessary to lie, cheat, and steal, (in the realm of cost reporting) so as to always be within budget, the budget that was always out of whack from the get-go because it had been built on the lying, cheating, and stealing done on the *last* job, and the jobs before that. Who knew how far back it might have gone?

I really considered it to be no big deal. I just continued to do my work with whatever means I had been provided and relied on the superintendent to cook my daily reports as he saw fit.

One day my crew and I were abruptly pulled from the area where we had been working and were rushed to the principal area of the project to complete what was a "critical path item." The irony of that was that neither the project management, the schedulers, nor the engineers seemed to have recognized that it was critical path until that very morning! But suddenly the rush was on.

Within a couple of hours I had tools and materials staged, and had carpenters sawing and pounding, and laborers fetching. But in the middle of it all I still had the project manager on his knees feverishly pouring over the drawings that were spread out on the ground in front of him. His face showed genuine concern as he nervously poked at the buttons of the pocket calculator he held in his hand. His attention shifted anxiously between the drawings and me, as he pointed out in excruciating detail just how many man hours had been allotted for each and every portion of the process, and how crucial it was that I get this work done on time, and hopefully within budget.

At one point, he glanced up and saw that I appeared to be daydreaming, and his response was swift. "You don't even care, do you?" he exclaimed with a sense of exasperation in his voice.

"No, not really," I replied.

"You *have* to care!" he almost shouted as he jumped to his feet. "It's a condition of your employment!"

"OK, I care!" was my muted response.

When that memory suddenly appeared in my consciousness some months ago, I simply smiled and noted it as one of those pleasant "on the job stories." As I pondered it for a moment however, I began to recognize some deeper significance. Much deeper.

As I was contemplating the difference between what the project manager thought I *should* care about and what I actually *did* care about, I suddenly recalled having remembered the "second question"; that memory had surfaced some months prior, and I could see some striking similarities. Please allow me to get to the second question by briefly revisiting the conversation that included not only that question, but the first one as well.

That conversation came as the result of having sent the woman in my life at the time to Al-Anon. The first question and its non-answer have been detailed earlier along with their profound effect on my life.

It was direct. "What are your goals?"

I can't imagine that there was much of a pause between that and the second question, and it was equally simple and direct: "What is your concept of God"?

I have no recollection of any response, nor of any particular reaction. That subject had been discounted and buried away for so long, it seems as though the question itself and any possible answers had simply been deflected without any consideration whatever.

When the memory of that second question suddenly surfaced a while ago, I had spent considerable time contemplating the significance of it, particularly the fact that it had remained unnoticed for well over twenty-five years.

As I pondered that, I realized that by the time I had found myself in Alcoholics Anonymous again, I was just ambivalent enough toward the traditional concepts of God that I was able to overlook most of the details of those concepts, and because for the first time in my life I really *did* want to not drink, I was able to simply trust the process, and begin to get involved in it. I don't really recall anyone poking me in the chest and telling me that I *had* to believe in God, but the implication was certainly there. They insinuated "you have to believe", and my reply was "OK I believe."

The coalition of these two seemingly totally unrelated stories is this: The project manager's assumption that I didn't care simply was not true. I *did* care. In fact, I cared deeply. I took great pride in my work; it was only my indifference to his intellectual and analytical *perception* of my work that had been problematic. Even though I had little interest in the company's methods and their over-analysis of everything, I was able to take care of my business without becoming overwhelmed and intimidated by their insistence that I pay strict attention to how it had allegedly been done in Omaha in 1896.

It was much the same in the early days of my sobriety. I *did* believe—not necessarily in the particulars of the dogma that they were preaching, but in the process itself, and the unexpected conviction that if I participated in all that, I may really have a chance to not drink and thus live a somewhat sensible life.

I *did* believe, just not in the details nor the specifics that everyone else seemed so sure of. Looking back now I can see that none of those differences were significant enough to be problematic.

It is the memory of another experience from my working days that really ties all of this together. Early in 2003 I was hired to be a part of the construction of Wynn Las Vegas, certainly the premier job in town, and possibly the entire country, at the time. Exciting stuff. However, I found myself working for the worst foremen I had ever encountered. Just a few weeks later he actually pulled me aside and very caustically said "You act like you don't even want to be here!"

I didn't really take time to think about it, and my response was unemotional and very direct, "That's just not true," I replied. "The fact is that I want to be on this job *more* than I *don't* want to work for you!"

So it was in the early days of my sobriety. I simply wanted to be sober more than I *didn't* want to do some of the seemingly ridiculous things folks were telling me that I had better do—or else.

ACRONYMIC

THE MEMBERS OF ALCOHOLICS ANONYMOUS seem to take great pleasure in shifting the acronymic process into reverse, thereby allowing them to create phrases and concepts that reflect the letters of a specific word. For example, EGO defines edging God out; YET indicates that you're eligible too. In keeping with that tradition, someone has actually taken the liberty of creating a couple of new gods! Good orderly direction and group of drunks are both recognized as reasonable substitutes for the "God of the preachers" that Bill referenced in his writings.

I have to seriously question the logic in that. If you truly do not believe that there is an interventionist deity who is capable of rearranging the circumstances of your life and will then alter your very human responses and reactions to those circumstances, how can you in good conscience acquiesce to either of those flimsy notions?

The fact is, I think most folks who subscribe to those surrogate deities would like to have their cake and eat it too. The idea that the solution must come from a Higher Power is so ingrained within the doctrine of AA that even those who do not accept the conventional concepts of God still feel obligated to profess a belief in *something*. I get the very strong impression that these folks do not think that it is possible to do AA without a reasonable replacement for the most fundamental aspect of Bill's dogma.

It would require mere seconds for me to name a dozen or more forces and/or entities that are more powerful than me, but I don't think that's the point. On page 45 *(Alcoholics Anonymous,)* Bill very clearly states what you can expect from this "*Power greater than ourselves*" (emphasis Bill's). He states that "that's exactly what this book is about. Its main object is to enable you to find a Power greater than yourself which will solve your problem." Try as I may, I just cannot imagine electricity, gravity, the wind, the ocean, the IRS, or the local police force fulfilling that expectation.

Common sense, (though it doesn't seem to be all that common as of yet), would indicate that alcoholism is not the mythic, supernatural demon that Bill envisioned and attempted to describe in his writings. I have written elsewhere about my opinions on the disease itself, they need not be revisited here. Suffice it to say however that without the supernatural demon, the need for a supernatural savior is diminished considerably.

In his quest to perpetuate the certainty of the need for some sort of divine intervention however, Bill seems to dismiss out of hand some of the most fundamentally useful aspects of Alcoholics Anonymous. One of the most glaring examples of that is on page 60 of *Alcoholics Anonymous* where he states in proposition

(b) (the second of the three pertinent ideas), *"that probably no human power could have relieved our alcoholism."*

If that were true, AA as we know it simply would not exist.

It may be semantics, or merely a shift away from the vernacular of AA, but I would like to suggest this: the quest for power is a non-starter. It is much more likely that we will realize the resolution of our dilemma by learning to recognize, and then utilize, the resources at hand.

One of the most readily available and certainly most helpful of these resources is the *human* resource that is the sobriety and collective wisdom of the members of AA.

To be fair, it should be pointed out that that resource was significantly smaller in the beginning, and consequently its value may not have been fully understood or appreciated. Fewer members, fewer opinions. Add to that the fact that AA's early association with the Oxford Group and their fundamentalist Christian doctrine had no doubt provided most of the early members with what they had considered to be the solution. Consequently, they likely paid less attention to the growing sense of community and the mutual strength that was rising in their relationships with each other.

The membership grew slowly, and there were barely a hundred (or so) sober alcoholics when the book *Alcoholics Anonymous* was published in 1939. I will be the first to give Bill credit for some of the incredible insight that he alludes to in some areas of the book, but I will also point out that the book was written as a promotional item to draw attention to the yet unnamed groups of drunks in New York City, and Akron, Ohio. To put it quite bluntly it was simply Bill's attempt to describe his own experience in such a way as to create interest in others.

Allow me this brief side note and let me point out that both of my grandfathers were born in 1895, the same year as Bill Wilson. In 1939 they were both farming tiny parcels of land with implements that were being drawn by horses. I cannot imagine digging through their diaries looking for clues on how best to run a dairy farm today.

My point is this: this is not your grandfather's AA.

Although there is still a cadre of "all the answers are in the book" folks around, they are not as predominate as they once were, and are therefore just a little less annoying.

The fact is that the miracle of Alcoholics Anonymous is alive and well and has not changed since the beginning—one drunk talking to another. One of the significant things that has changed is the diversity of the membership. Today there are a wide variety of thoughts and opinions about the essence of what it is to be an alcoholic, and more importantly what it is to be one that does not drink.

As it turns out, the association with a group of drunks, and recognizing the worth of some good orderly direction are both extremely valuable assets, but I don't think either one of them need qualify as a viable "Higher Power."

FORMER AGNOSTIC

I AM QUITE AMUSED BY those that claim to be former agnostics. It's likely that more than just a few of them have used the label "agnostic" as a smoke screen to avoid admitting that they were simply not interested in playing by the rules.

Engaging in behavior that is socially questionable and religiously taboo, would be much easier if those social and religious guidelines were dismissed as irrelevant; and by disclaiming belief in the deity that has reputedly mandated those moral codes, ignoring them would certainly seem to be much less consequential.

This feigned agnosticism is nothing more than a psychological trick that allows one to sit on the fence just in case the day may arrive when the possible consequences of one's actions have become frightening enough to get off said fence and begin the attempt to squeeze through the repentance loophole.

The loophole that Alcoholics Anonymous provides is the "as we understood him" loophole—, and what an enormous loophole it is! Over the years I have heard some truly incredible claims regarding the liberal use of that concept. The only consistency seems to be that the alternate deity be capable of intervening in one's

life and also be willing to manipulate the circumstances surrounding that life.

Bill notes in his story *(Alcoholics Anonymous p. 12)*
that Ebby had offered this suggestion: "*Why don't you
choose your own concept of God?*" That idea, however,
has been seriously diluted over the years and has actually morphed into the notion that you can *create* your
own concept of God.

I have heard many members offer this advice to
newer folks that seem to be struggling with the "God
idea."

The instructions are actually quite simple: Take a
sheet of paper and draw a vertical line down the center
of it. On one side list all the characteristics that you
don't like about God, and on the other side list all that
you do. Now tear the sheet down the middle and keep
only the half that lists your favorable concepts of God.
That can be your Higher Power!

Take a moment and let the irrationality of that settle in.

The twentieth-century Indian sage Sri Nisargadatta
Maharaj offers this opinion on that concept:

> "The God born of fear and hope, then shaped
> by desire and imagination, simply cannot be,
> the Power that is all; the heart and mind of the
> universe."

The intent of this piece is not to belittle, or poke fun
at, what I consider to be the absurdity of some folk's
beliefs. In fact, I think for some people the silliness

itself is what is attractive about some of those concepts. In AA speak, these ideas are the "easier softer way"—they require little critical thinking, and even less logic. The thinking seems to be this: "OK I got me a higher power, let's check that box and move on."

However, if I *were* to identify the intent of this piece, I suppose I would describe it as this: to dispel some of the common misconceptions about agnosticism, or at the very least offer my own experience and understanding of an agnostic point of view.

There is no need to get too deeply into a biography of Thomas Huxley, who first coined the term agnostic, but the following excerpt from his 1889 essay "Agnosticism" is Huxley's own account of how and why he had come to use the term some twenty years earlier.

"When I reached intellectual maturity and began to ask myself whether I was an atheist, a theist, or a pantheist; a materialist or an idealist; Christian or a freethinker; I found that the more I learned and reflected, the less ready was the answer; until, at last, I came to the conclusion that I had neither art nor part with any of these denominations, except the last. The one thing in which most of these good people were agreed was the one thing in which I differed from them. They were quite sure they had attained a certain 'gnosis,'—had, more or less successfully, solved the problem of existence; while I was quite sure I had not, and had a pretty strong conviction that the problem was insoluble."

Huxley further defined agnosticism as a method or a practice, not a *creed* or just another *ism*. It is literally the *"way* of not knowing." He referred to it as the *"agnostic faith",* the faith and confidence that it is legitimate to not know, to not subscribe to any particular set of rules and meanings.

That is certainly contrary to the contemporary perception that agnosticism is nothing more than a lackadaisical attitude toward God and/or religion. I actually know a couple of anti-theists whose opinion it is that agnostics are simply too lazy to be good atheists.

Agnostic means that I don't know, not that I don't care. I really wonder just how many self-proclaimed agnostics actually fall into the latter category. By the same token, I suspect that the same could be said for many of the folks who claim to be "spiritual but not religious." Simply eschewing organized religion does not automatically place one on a spiritual path.

Agnosticism is most often linked, (and quite unfairly in my opinion), to atheism, and therefore is generally assumed to be simply a contrarian perspective of traditional theological points of view. That may well be true for some, but that has not been my path at all. I have realized my sense of being from questioning *everything*. Theologians are certainly not the only group of folks who are stubborn and dogmatic about their beliefs.

The depth of a radically agnostic point of view does not come exclusively from questioning other people's opinions and their more traditional points of view, however. Huxley's "pretty strong conviction that the problem is insoluble" really is the foundation.

The gradual realization that there simply are no answers for the most fundamental of questions brings enormous relief, but that in no way dampens my curiosity. Now we're back to what I consider to be the human dilemma: the insatiable desire to figure things out, and the nagging suspicion that we're failing miserably in our efforts to do so.

That enigmatic drive that seems to be inherently woven into our DNA is the churning of opposites that moves us forward in the evolutionary process: the increasingly astounding discoveries on the one hand, and the ever-present suspicion that it's never enough on the other.

The certainty that somehow, some way, some day "it" (regardless of how you define it) can be known, is the fuel that keeps the unquenchable thirst burning.

Perhaps the most valued aspect of the "don't know mind" is the gradual realization that the mystery of the human dilemma need not be solved. The fervent hope that it can be, or someday will be, is an illusion.

That realization can still be quite unsettling, however. It may feel as though you are abandoning the very essence of life itself. The temptation to put the blinders back on and return to the treadmill is compelling. With some patience, however, you may gradually realize that it is possible to live life as it is currently unfolding, rather than being caught up in the constant anticipation of how it may or may not unfold in the future.

I point regularly to the stillness that has been so fundamental to my sense of being. I recognize today that a very large part of that stillness has come as a result of letting go of the need to know and the incessant urge to figure things out. Most importantly, I no longer find myself in search of something to believe in.

What remains is the absolute joy of continuous wonder. I still wonder about a lot of the same things I have always wondered about, but the joy is revealed to be the wonder itself, not the finding of any answers. Without the need for resolution, this realization gently dawns: I am not the one who is seeking a solution to the mystery—I *am* the mystery. Just typing those words brings a smile to my face and a gladness to my heart.

So allow me to now return to my original sense of amusement, and ask this question: Why would anyone who had tasted the liberation and freedom of a truly open mind, ever choose to return to the "I know" mind of adolescence, and then renew their search for a collection of fairy tales to console themselves with?

Former agnostic? I seriously doubt it.

JUMPING TO CONCLUSIONS

ONE OF MY FAVORITE REFERENCES to some "other power" is the "unsuspected inner resource" that Bill alludes to in the second appendix of the book *Alcoholic Anonymous*. It is presented there in the context of his attempt to allay the expectations of those who assumed (based on his own experience and his description of it), that this "spiritual awakening" was some sort of white light/burning bush experience. For the most part he does a reasonable job of that; however, as is quite often the case, he projects his own opinions and beliefs about that resource onto "most of us."

He goes even further in stating his opinion about the matter on page 55 *(Alcoholics Anonymous)* where he asserts that "deep down in *every* man, woman, and child is the fundamental idea of God." (emphasis mine). If I were to accuse Bill of being presumptuous, that statement would be exhibit A.

Allow me to rekindle some childhood memories. Do you remember using the "everyone's doing it" logic on your parents? Their rebuttal quite often included a question like this: "Well, if Billy jumps off a bridge are you simply going to follow him?" Consider that question rhetorical, but this one is similar: If Billy jumps to the conclusion that that sense of "something other" is the fundamental idea of God, that is to say *his* idea of God, are you obliged to follow?

I have often quipped that before my late wife passed, I had been married to a world-class athlete. If the International Olympic Committee had ever sanctioned the "jumping to conclusions" event, she would have been right there, among the world's best, and Bill Wilson could certainly have received some consideration.

One of the more curious attitudes that has evolved since the founding of Alcoholics Anonymous, (in the minds of the traditionalists at least,) is that Bill Wilson personally had, and/or that AA in general has, all the answers. I would suggest that, in no small part, that mindset comes from decades of having followed Bill blindly as he jumped from one conclusion to another.

He tells us on page 45 *(Alcoholics Anonymous)* "exactly what this book is about." Let's begin this adventure with the paragraph that precedes that statement.

"Lack of power, that was our dilemma."

That is the conclusion that Bill had come to, based on his understanding of the fundamental predicament. That conclusion, of course, led to the *final* conclusion— that the solution to that dilemma had to be some other power, a power greater than ourselves. His ensuing description and portrayal of it leaves little doubt as to what he considered that power to be.

However, since there seems to be thousands of alcoholics who have found lasting and perfectly comfortable sobriety without the need to offer suppli-cation to a cosmic boss begging for some sort of divine intervention on their behalf, I am willing to come right out and say that the second conclusion is false; or at the very least not absolutely true.

If the second conclusion loses some of its supreme merit, perhaps we should take a closer look at the dilemma itself as it is stated in the first conclusion.

Lack of understanding describes that dilemma much more accurately. Lack of understanding is the genesis of most, if not *all*, human dilemmas. The lack of under-standing is grounded in a shortage of facts—insuffi-cient knowledge.

Bill, or anyone else in the years prior to any mod-ern medical research, was limited in both facts and knowledge about this mysterious quandary defined as alcoholism.

I think we would do well to back up a bit in the his-tory of our cultures and recognize that it has not been that many years since humans were willing to credit any one of a wide variety of super-natural forces for circumstances that were beyond logical explanation. For better or worse.

Add to that the remnants of the theistic notion that lingers, in our culture at least, that there is a titanic battle that rages endlessly between the forces of good and evil, and you get to the perspective from which Bill viewed and therefore described the dilemma.

Based on my perusal of Bill's writings, I would have to question whether he ever got over the idea of "King

Alcohol" being some sort of nefarious mythic force from the dark side that he would be obliged to grapple with interminably.

If you sift carefully through the process of recovery as viewed from his perspective, it becomes apparent that in his view, the conflict is pervasive, and can never be abandoned. At every turn there is something more that must be overcome, and he seems to assume that every bit of it is responsible for alcoholism. Thus, the old formula is introduced again and again; the powerlessness is universal, as is the need for continuous dependence upon the intervention of that external source of power.

Little wonder he was convinced that he needed a higher power—a *much* higher power!

Let me be clear; it's not the notion of powerlessness itself that I am questioning, it is the inference of the never-ending battle that must be waged and can never be won; and the perception that the enemy cannot be so much as held at bay without deference to some supreme being. That is what I take exception to.

With the acceptance of just a bare minimum of evidence that alcoholism has a physiological component, and the willingness to reevaluate the wording of the first step, we can come to a much more logical assessment of the overall problem, i.e., I am not powerless over *alcohol* at all, what I am powerless over is what happens in my body when I ingest it.

So, alcohol per se is not the problem, it is my drinking! Bill was well aware of that; in fact he pointed it out on p. 64 *(Alcoholics Anonymous)* : "Our liquor was but a symptom, we had to get down to causes and conditions."

I am in total agreement with that evaluation. Therefore, it is my opinion that the solution is not to be found in winning the battle against alcohol, it is found through the investigation into, and the resolution of, those causes and conditions; and that is the efficacy of the steps.

Now about those steps. A review of them as they are written clearly reveals Bill's concept of the process:

- Find God
- Confess your sins
- Repent
- Receive communion
- And then, having renewed your covenant, live happily ever after.

The sticking points would seem to be in the happily ever after part. There is some fine print in that contract (covenant).

I am reminded of a burst of clarity that came to me several years ago while gathered with a group of friends that had for several weeks been reading and discussing a book written by Sam Harris. The book describes the possibility of awakening to a spiritual path without the need for any beliefs. Although he is considered by many to be one of the "modern atheists," Mr. Harris is not shy about his views on spirituality.

One of the regular members of our book group had invited another of his friends, an exceptionally strong believer, to join us. This fellow strained the discussions regularly with his religious dogma. After several weeks of prattle about just wanting to please God, he slipped one day and admitted that his real concern was about not saying or doing anything that would *displease* God.

I think even he was astounded when he recognized the difference that he had just identified.

In my opinion that is the mindset of nervousness and fear that Bill presents in his writings.

Grace, by its most religious definition, is seen as the unmerited favor of God. If you accept that belief, you are left beholden. Even the slightest misstep in your life places you in jeopardy of that grace being withdrawn, and your finding yourself once again an outcast. With that very frightening proposition as the driving force, the nervousness about preserving your foothold on the tightrope is unrelenting, and the ongoing struggle continues to churn, seemingly without end.

Fortunately, I have some good news; it is in fact exceptionally good news. Even though I have seen innumerable folks over the years who seem to have embraced Bill's perspective of the process wholeheartedly and therefore appear to be stuck with a very tenuous view of their sobriety, that does not *have* to be the result of these steps.

Bill identifies the first step in recovery on page 30, *(Alcoholics Anonymous)*. "We learned that we had to fully concede to our innermost selves that we were alcoholic." I think a sense of agreement most accurately describes that concession. To come into agreement with being an alcoholic and looking honestly at what that means, is to also come into agreement with taking the steps necessary to literally alter the course of your life.

If you have found yourself with your nose poked into Alcoholics Anonymous, you have no doubt noticed that these good folks have already published a set of steps for your convenience. (Please note that they have been offered as suggestions. Not all of the evangelical members remember that.)

Over the years I have heard many members abridge the first three of those steps into these three simple ideas: I can't, He can, I think I'll let Him. I like the brevity of that but have simplified them even further by eliminating the intervention of a deity: I can't, *we* can, I think I'll participate.

The initial phases of this process need be no more complicated than that. The willingness to participate is the key.

I am going to venture way outside the lines now and suggest that the remainder of the process can be viewed much more realistically as a continuum rather than a linear cause and effect progression.

The traditional mindset has been that the steps are numbered for a reason and should be done in order. There may have been some merit to that idea at one time, and that may remain useful for some, but I don't find that to be particularly valid.

The language Bill used to describe the fourth step creates dread at the very outset. My mind cannot wrap itself around fearless without recognizing fear, and the very thought of moral puts me on the fast track back to preadolescent Sunday School. Add to that all the drama from the stories about the months required to compile dozens of pages of inventory, and hours and hours of fifth step work that is heard about in meetings, and it's little wonder that people balk. If viewed from the "do 'em in order" school of thought, the whole process can easily grind to a screeching halt.

I am not suggesting that getting involved with the remainder of the steps should be delayed however, in fact, quite the opposite. What I am suggesting is a different approach. Ideally the willingness to participate will include taking some of the standard suggestions such as lots of meetings, sponsorship, (or at least some developing friendships), fundamental commitments and so on.

But I don't think it's ever too early to introduce the basics of a meditation practice. The most fundamental aspect of that is to begin to pay attention, which is the foundation of step ten. That is aided significantly by learning to take a moment to simply pause, taking a time-out from the seemingly endless chatter that races through one's mind. Those brief moments of respite can be cultivated into a wonderful stillness, and regardless of how brief those moments are, that is the very essence of step eleven. The culmination of these efforts is most often referred to as mindfulness.

One of the most important aspects of this mindfulness is the recognition of just how often and how quickly we react to, and jump to conclusions about, thoughts that randomly appear in our minds, often with disastrous results.

I doubt that very many people ever slow down enough to actually think about their thinking. Some disciplines would suggest that you simply need to become aware of your thoughts, but that barely scratches the surface. If we are truly getting down to causes and conditions, we need to go deeper than that. Questioning these thoughts can be most revealing. The questions could be many; Is that true? Do I really believe that, and if so, why? Let me be extremely facetious and once again quote Bill here. "If we are painstaking about this phase of our development, we will be amazed before we are halfway through." *(Alcoholics Anonymous p. 83)*

In a roundabout way Bill himself actually alludes to this sort of inquiry on page 58 *(Alcoholics Anonymous)* where he states, "Some of us have tried to hold on to our old ideas and the result was nil till we let go absolutely."

All this brings me to perhaps the most valuable aspect of this entire mindful point of view; the realization that Bill was absolutely right in this assessment stated on page 62 *(Alcoholics Anonymous)*: "So our troubles, we think, are basically of our own making."

When I first read that I had assumed, and possibly with good reason, that what Bill was referring to was the chaos that had followed me through the doors of AA. As I began to investigate the nature of my mind and the process of my thinking however, I began to see that the vast majority of those troubles were generated by my believing things that simply were not true including my own thoughts.

By learning to question our thinking we can begin to view the circumstances of our lives from a completely different perspective, and as a result the process of the steps takes on a completely new meaning. As it unfolds, the mistakes and misadventures identified and discussed in steps four and five, and the amends that are contemplated and executed in steps eight and nine, almost seem to triage themselves into their own order of significance. Most importantly each item can be addressed in its own time and separately from the rest, allowing us to return repeatedly to the stillness of ten and eleven. A little contemplation on this process is likely to reveal that it is not the onus of getting sober, it is much more akin to creating the experience of being sober.

If lack of understanding is in fact the dilemma, then the quest to understand becomes the path to recovery. It would seem then, that understanding alcoholism itself would surely be at the top of the list, followed closely by Alcoholics Anonymous, then the steps, and most likely the rest of the ritual as well.

If you are paying attention however, you will begin to see that all that focus is misplaced. Coming to an

understanding of our selves is what is of utmost importance, and that is in fact the objective of the steps.

The most utterly amazing reality of this whole
adventure is this: As we recognize and let go of all the
false concepts of who we *think* we are, we find ourselves coming more and more into alignment with
who we really are.

And much to our own amazement we realize that we
are that "unsuspected inner resource."

ABOUT THE AUTHOR

WES STILL LIVES IN LAS VEGAS, and even though his wife passed a few years ago he is perfectly content with caring for a couple of aging cats and communing with a wonderful collection of like-minded people. He continues to spend an inordinate amount of his time contemplating how best to describe his journey, and smiling at the Taoist wisdom that suggests "the way that can be named is not the eternal way."